French Cookery

French Cookery

HELGE RUBINSTEIN

Illustrated by Tony Streek

Eyre Methuen London

First published 1979
by Eyre Methuen Ltd
11 New Fetter Lane, London EC4P 4EE

Copyright © 1979 by Helge Rubinstein

ISBN 0 413 38230 3

Printed in Great Britain by
Hazell Watson & Viney Ltd
Aylesbury, Bucks

Contents

CONTENTS 9

Introduction

Few people would deny French cooking its pre-eminent
position in the world of gastronomy, but it is wrong to think
that it need be either élitist or esoteric. There are the great
names of haute cuisine – maître-chefs of grand hotels and
owners of rosetted *tables* – and there are also everyday or
domestic practitioners of French cooking. This book cele-
brates the art and skills of housewives rather than of high
priests. You will find in the pages that follow most of the
famous dishes of the classic repertoire, but by no means all. I
have omitted those that involve exorbitantly dear items such
as lobsters or truffles, or require resources of time and talents

which can only normally be achieved in a restaurant kitchen, with its vast *batterie de cuisine*, its countless *fonds* for elaborate sauces and many hands for decorating the food – and for washing-up!

This book, then, is about *La cuisine bourgeoise*, such as a French housewife might cook for her family, though the recipes have been adapted for use by her English counterpart, with ingredients which are readily available in this country. Some are unashamedly luxurious, for special occasions, others make the most of inexpensive foods, for the French *bonne femme* is probably more economical of ingredients than of her time.

Not that the French housewife is tied to her stove these days, as perhaps her mother used to be. She will often combine a job with her role in the home, and has learned to make good use of convenience foods and such aids to relaxed housekeeping as the freezer. Frozen foods, for instance, are as common now in French supermarkets as they are over here, and many of the recipes in this book suggest the kind of shortcuts that the use of frozen products allows.

France is so vast and so rich in natural resources that her cooking is still very regional. It is outside the scope of this book to do proper justice to the individual flavour of these regional cuisines, but I hope nonetheless that the reader will be able to pick up some whiff of the fundamental differences in character between, say, a dish from Normandy, with its emphasis on apples, cream and butter, and one from Provence making use of such characteristic local products of the Midi as garlic, tomatoes and olive oil.

It would be graceless to write a French cookbook without some mention of the giants in the field, to whom I can only acknowledge my lifelong debt. First and foremost to Elizabeth David, for her great qualities of inspiration; then to Tante Marie, the French Mrs Beeton, for her blessed simplicity, and finally to Julia Child, for her meticulous step-by-step instructions. I hope that anyone to whom this book has proved an appetite whetter, will go on to search further among these and others.

This book is not meant to be a comprehensive guide, but

more a personal anthology. Were it not part of a series, I would have liked to call it 'An Introduction to French cooking for those who love to cook'. Bon appétit!

Helge Rubinstein.

Ingredients

Butter French butter, especially from Normandy and Brittany, is usually unsalted or only very slightly salted. Where this matters, I have specified that unsalted butter should be used. If it is difficult to obtain, you can clarify salted butter by melting it down until it just begins to foam, and then straining into a bowl to cool. Most of the salty particles will remain in the strainer, and the rest can be scraped off the top of the butter when it has set. There will also be a milky residue left under the butter in the bottom of the bowl, which may be added to soups or sauces.

This clarified butter is also useful for frying, as it does not burn as easily as salted butter.

Bouquet Garni is a bunch of herbs which should be tied together before adding to the dish, and removed before serving. A classic bouquet consists of a few sprigs of parsley, a bayleaf and a sprig of thyme, to which a small sprig of rosemary may also be added. If fresh herbs are not available, dried ones may be used instead, but they should, strictly speaking, be tied in a piece of muslin or cheesecloth, so that they can be removed. Some herb firms market small muslin bags of bouquets garnis.

Lightly Soured Cream CREME FRAICHE

French cream, known as crème fraîche, is left to mature so that the lactic acids in it remain active and give it a very slightly sour flavour. The butterfat content is much the same as that of our double cream.

It is particularly good for cooking, as it gives a slight tang, rather as sour cream does, but is a better thickener than the latter. Double cream can always be substituted for crème fraîche in a recipe, but it is also quite easy to make crème fraîche yourself.

280ml ($\frac{1}{2}$ pint, 1$\frac{1}{4}$ cups US) double cream	*1 tablespoon sour cream or buttermilk*

Stir the sour cream or buttermilk into the double cream, and heat very gently till lukewarm. The temperature must not be allowed to exceed 29C, 85F. (It should still feel slightly cool to the back of a finger.) Pour into a bowl, cover and leave in a warm place to thicken. This will take anything from 5 to 24 hours, depending on the temperature.

The cream will now keep for at least 10 days in the refrigerator.

Crème Chantilly

Crème Chantilly is whipped crème fraîche, and whipped double or whipping cream can therefore always be used instead.

As crème fraîche becomes very thick on beating, it is necessary to add between ¼ and ⅓ as much iced water to the cream before it can be whipped. This makes it very light, as well as being very slightly sour, and these two characteristics of crème chantilly make it especially good with very sweet or rich desserts. Sweeten the cream only very lightly, if at all.

Note : Stiffly beaten egg white is sometimes added to give it extra lightness and bulk.

Garlic Though it is sometimes thought to be omnipresent in the French cuisine, garlic is actually used with discrimination and discretion by good cooks. I have included it in the list of ingredients wherever it is a vital addition to the flavour of a dish. You can of course omit it, but I would beg you to try it at least once in those recipes where it appears.

Oil Olive oil has a very special flavour, and is vital to some dishes, mostly those coming from the South. Where this is so, I have specified olive oil in the list of ingredients and 'real' olive oil, not the refined variety to be bought in chemist shops, should be used. Elsewhere, a less highly flavoured oil, such as corn or vegetable oils, may be used, either alone, or in combination with olive oil. It is a matter of taste, and I have therefore left it to the discretion of the cook.

Pastry In France, as in England, there are two basic kinds of pastry, the puff pastry or *pâte feuilletée*, and the short crust or *pâte brisée*. I have not given instructions for making the former, as these are available in any standard cookery book, and the French does not differ from the English recipe.

Moreover, the readily available frozen puff pastries are now so good, that all but the most ambitious cooks will probably settle for using these.
Recipes for French shortcrust pastry are given below:

Shortcrust Pastry PATE BRISEE

This is the basic French shortcrust pastry, to be used for quiches and tarts. It is lighter and crisper than its English counterpart, and also more fragile, and must be handled as little and as lightly as possible.
This quantity makes approximately 400g (14oz) of pastry, sufficient to line two 25–30cm (10–12in) flan tins.

140g (5oz) plain white flour
a pinch of salt
a pinch of icing sugar

110g (4oz) butter, preferably unsalted
scant 100ml ($\frac{1}{2}$ gill, $\frac{3}{8}$ cup US) cold water

Sift the flour on to a pastry board, and sprinkle on the salt and sugar. Cut in the butter with a palette knife into small pieces, then crumble lightly with the tips of the fingers until the mixture resembles coarse breadcrumbs. Sprinkle on the water, and quickly gather together into a ball with one hand. Sprinkle the board with a little more flour, then quickly spread the pastry away from you on to the floured board, bit by bit, with the heel of the hand. This ensures that the butter is evenly distributed. The whole operation should be done as quickly and lightly as possible, and should not take more than a few minutes. Gather up the dough into a ball again and chill on a plate or in a polythene bag for one hour before using.
The dough will keep in the refrigerator for at least one week, and indefinitely in the freezer.
When ready to use, roll out very lightly, working from the centre outwards. If the dough is very hard at first, bang it a little with the rolling pin, but do not knead again.

Variation

Sweetened Shortcrust Pastry PATE BRISEE SUCREE

A sweeter version of this pastry is often used for fruit tarts. The ingredients and method are exactly the same as above, but instead of only a pinch of sugar, sprinkle 60g (2oz) of caster or icing sugar over the flour before you begin.

Wine The French use a great deal of wine in their cooking, though often only in small quantities. Some people keep a regular supply of cooking wine, others prefer to use leftovers when possible, or else to take what is required from a bottle that is to be drunk with the meal. Occasionally, the type and quality of the wine is really important, and where this is so, I have specified it in the recipe. Obviously, the better the wine, the better the end result, but even quite rough cooking wine, properly reduced, will enhance a dish.

Glossary

I have avoided using technical terms wherever possible, but there are three instances where the use of a single word or phrase can save lengthy description.

Bain-Marie Some foods need long slow cooking, and the bain-marie is a device for keeping them at just about simmering point. You can buy a special bain-marie pan, but a baking tin or large saucepan will serve equally well. Where a recipe suggests the use of a bain-marie, place the dish in a large baking-tin containing water. The water should come about half-way up the dish, and may need topping up from time to time. This process ensures that such dishes as pâté are cooked through evenly, and will prevent a crème renversée, for example, from curdling.

Baking Blind describes the preliminary baking of a pastry case before the filling is added. It is important to stop the pastry from bubbling up too much during this process. The pastry should always be well pricked and it is best also to weight it down. Use crumpled foil, or some dried haricot beans which can be kept especially for this purpose and used over and over again. Small metal beans can also be bought from sophisticated kitchen shops.

Beurre Manié is a combination of butter and flour used to thicken sauces and soups. Combine equal quantities of softened butter and flour to make a thick paste, and stir small quantities of this into the sauce or soup until they reach the required consistency. This method is guaranteed to thicken without producing any lumps.

Quantities and Measurements

Quantities given in this book are for four people – in so far as it is possible to lay down how much people should or do eat! However, there are occasions when it is not possible or sensible to cook in these quantities, and in those cases I have said so.

Measurements have been given in metric and imperial units and American cups. Sometimes strict accuracy is vital, at other times it has seemed more important to bear in mind how the particular ingredient is likely to be bought, and 4oz, for instance, may therefore be given as 100g in one recipe, and as 125g in another.

Starters • Les Hors D'Oeuvres

Even the simplest French meal is likely to begin with an hors d'oeuvre, a pâté or a soup. The hors d'oeuvre may be no more than a few slices of local sausage or small fresh, or even tinned, fish, attractively laid out on a plate with some olives or radishes. Whether it consists of one or more ingredients, they will always be carefully chosen to go with each other – nowhere in France will you find the 'hors d'oeuvre varié' so beloved of English restaurants, where an ill-chosen variety of meat, fish, egg and vegetables lie as uneasy bedfellows on a bed of limp lettuce.

The hors d'oeuvre is designed to take the first edge off the appetite, and yet also to whet it, so it should always be served in small quantities and will often be rather sharp in taste. In France, it is invariably accompanied by crusty French bread and butter.

Globe Artichokes

LES ARTICHAUTS

1 artichoke per person

Wash the artichokes and leave them steeped in plenty of salted cold water for 15–20 minutes to clean. Cut the stalks off close to the base. Plunge into a large saucepan of boiling salted water and boil steadily until they are cooked. This may take anything from 25–45 minutes or longer, depending on the size and freshness of the artichokes. You can tell when they are cooked by pulling out one of the leaves – if it comes out easily, and its base is tender, the artichokes are ready. Pour off the water, and leave the artichokes upside down to drain.

They may be served hot or cold, with a number of different sauces.

For special occasions, remove the 'choke' before serving. Gently open up the leaves from the centre until you can reach the hairy small spikes of the choke. Pluck these out gently or scrape out with a teaspoon, bit by bit, then close the artichoke up again, or leave opened up and serve with a little sauce poured into the centre. For lesser occasions, let each person deal with his own choke. Serve little pots of the chosen sauce so that everyone can dip their leaves in one by one.

Serve hot with a sauce hollandaise, béarnaise or mousseline (see pp. 47, 48) or simply some butter lightly melted, so that it is creamy but not oily, to which you have added lemon juice, seasoning and some finely chopped mixed fresh herbs.

Serve cold with a sauce vinaigrette or ravigotte, or a light mayonnaise (see pp. 48, 51, 52).

Note : For those who have never eaten an artichoke, here is how to eat it : starting from the outside, pull off each leaf one by one, holding it by the tip, dip it in the sauce, then pull the base of the leaf through the teeth, so that you eat the fleshy bottom part of the leaf, with its coating of sauce, and discard the remains of the leaf. When you reach the base of the artichoke, after removing the choke, eat this with a knife and fork – it is the best part.

Shrimps in Brandy Sauce

CREVETTES EN COCOTTE

If shrimps are not available, or you find them too fiddly, use prawns instead.

1 litre (2 pints, 5 cups US) shrimps or prawns in their shells
strip of lemon peel
1 small onion or shallot
tarragon, fennel, parsley
60g (2oz) butter

30g (1oz) flour
1 teaspoon tomato purée
squeeze of lemon juice
salt and freshly ground black pepper
1 tablespoon thick double cream
1 tablespoon brandy or sherry

Shell the shrimps or prawns and put the shells in a large saucepan. Cover with cold water, add the lemon peel, onion and herbs and boil fast, without a lid, for 10 minutes. Strain and set aside.

Meanwhile toss the shrimps or prawns in the butter for 5 minutes over a gentle heat. Sprinkle on the flour, and cook gently, stirring, for 3 minutes. Add the tomato purée and then slowly add 280ml ($\frac{1}{2}$ pint) of the strained stock from the shells. When the mixture is quite thick and smooth, add the lemon juice, season to taste, stir in the cream and the brandy or sherry, heat through well and serve in small cocotte or ramekin dishes.

Raw Vegetable Hors D'Oeuvre

LES CRUDITES

This can be the simplest hors d'oeuvre of all, and at the right time of the year, in early summer, quite the most delectable.

Choose a selection of any number of young, fresh vegetables – carrots, cucumber, celery, beans or peas (very young broad beans or peas are delicious eaten whole, in the pod), radishes, fennel, florets of cauliflower, peppers, red or green, and small firm tomatoes.

Serve the vegetables whole, or, if more appropriate, sliced; plain, with plenty of seasalt to hand for dunking, or with one or a selection of sauces, such as any kind of mayonnaise, a rouille or a tapenade (see pp. 30, 48, 50).

Sardine Puffs

DARTOIS DE SARDINES

200g (7oz) puff pastry
1 120g (4¼oz) tin sardines in oil
salt and freshly ground black
  pepper

1 tablespoon lemon juice
1 egg
1 tablespoon milk

Roll out the puff pastry ¼cm (⅛in) thick and cut into 10cm (4in) squares.

Remove the backbones and tails from the sardines and mash them with a fork, blending in the lemon juice and seasoning. Place a teaspoonful of the mixture on each square, fold them over to make triangles and seal and crimp the edges. Beat the egg and milk together with a fork and brush liberally onto each triangle. Bake in a hot oven (220C, 425F, Mark 7) for 20–25 minutes, until the puffs have risen and are golden brown. Serve hot.

This quantity makes about 8–10 puffs.

Variation : Lightly flaked tuna fish may be used instead of sardines.

Cold Vegetables Stewed in Olive Oil

LEGUMES A LA GRECQUE

In spite of their name, vegetables cooked in this way provide a typical, simple French hors d'oeuvre. Almost any crisp vegetable may be cooked in this way (leeks, pimento, fennel or aubergine are all excellent cooked according to one of the following recipes) but the three given below are perhaps the most frequently encountered. Serve any one of them on their own, or in any combination.

Mushrooms Stewed in Olive Oil

CHAMPIGNONS A LA GRECQUE

For this you should really use tiny, unopened button mushrooms. Slightly larger ones may be halved or quartered, but the open, flat variety of mushroom should not be used.

500g (1lb) button mushrooms
140ml ($\frac{1}{4}$ pint, $\frac{5}{8}$ cup US) water
140ml ($\frac{1}{4}$ pint, $\frac{5}{8}$ cup US) white wine
juice of $\frac{1}{2}$ lemon
4 tablespoons olive oil
6 peppercorns, lightly crushed

6 coriander seeds, lightly crushed
bayleaf
sprig of thyme
pinch of sugar
salt
parsley

Wash or wipe the mushrooms, trim them but do not peel.

Put all the other ingredients, except for the parsley, of which only 1 sprig should be used, into a saucepan, bring to the boil and simmer for 5 minutes. Add the mushrooms, cover and simmer for 5 minutes, or until they are just tender. Lift the mushrooms out with a slotted spoon and place in a serving dish. Boil the liquid rapidly for 5 minutes to reduce, remove the bayleaf, and the sprigs of thyme and parsley and pour over the mushrooms. Taste for seasoning and leave to cool.

Serve when cold, sprinkled with some freshly chopped parsley.

Courgettes Stewed in Olive Oil

COURGETTES A LA GRECQUE

500g (1lb) courgettes	$\frac{1}{2}$ teaspoon coriander seeds,
280ml ($\frac{1}{2}$ pint, 1$\frac{1}{4}$ cups US) water	lightly crushed
4 tablespoons olive oil	1 clove garlic, lightly crushed
juice of $\frac{1}{2}$ lemon	salt
bayleaf	$\frac{1}{2}$ teaspoon sugar
sprig of thyme	1 tablespoon tomato purée
6 peppercorns, lightly crushed	225g ($\frac{1}{2}$lb) tomatoes

Wash or wipe the courgettes, trim off the ends, but do not peel. Slice thickly, place in a colander and sprinkle with salt. Leave to drain for about one hour.

Put all the remaining ingredients apart from the tomatoes into a saucepan, bring to the boil and simmer for 5 minutes. Then add the drained courgettes and the tomatoes, peeled and roughly chopped. Simmer over a moderate heat, uncovered, for 20–25 minutes, until the courgettes are tender and the sauce almost evaporated. Remove the bayleaf and sprig of thyme, pour into a serving dish and serve chilled.

Onions Stewed in Olive Oil

OIGNONS A LA GRECQUE

450g (1lb) button or pickling onions	2 tablespoons concentrated tomato purée
140ml ($\frac{1}{4}$ pint, $\frac{5}{8}$ cup US) water	12 peppercorns, lightly crushed
140ml ($\frac{1}{4}$ pint, $\frac{5}{8}$ cup US) red wine	6 coriander seeds, lightly crushed
juice of $\frac{1}{2}$ lemon	1 sprig rosemary
4 tablespoons olive oil	1 sprig thyme
2 tablespoons sugar	bayleaf
	parsley
	salt

Peel the onions and blanch them for 1 minute in boiling water.

Put all the rest of the ingredients, except for all but one sprig of the parsley, into a saucepan, bring to the boil and simmer for 5 minutes. Add the drained onions, cover and simmer for 20–30 minutes, or until the onions are tender but have not lost their shape.

Lift the onions out with a slotted spoon and place on a serving dish. Bring the liquid quickly to the boil, and boil rapidly for 5–10 minutes, until it is much reduced and quite thick. Remove the bayleaf and the sprigs of rosemary, thyme and parsley and pour over the onions. Leave to cool.

Serve when cold, sprinkled with some freshly chopped parsley.

Celeriac Salad

REMOULADE DE CELERI-RAVE

1 medium celeriac root (approx. 500g, 1lb)	*1 tablespoon boiling water*
	2 tablespoons oil
juice of ½ lemon	*1 teaspoon wine vinegar*
salt	*salt and pepper*
2 tablespoons French mustard	*parsley*

Peel the celeriac and grate coarsely or cut into fine Julienne strips. Sprinkle with the lemon juice and salt, mix well and leave to marinade for ½ hour.

Whisk the boiling water into the French mustard, then slowly beat in the oil, drop by drop, as for making mayonnaise. When the sauce is thick and creamy, beat in the wine vinegar, season to taste, and fold into the celeriac, together with some finely chopped parsley. Mix very well so that all the celeriac is coated with the sauce.

Mushroom Salad with Cream

SALADE DE CHAMPIGNONS A LA CREME

250g (½lb) white button
  mushrooms
lemon juice
140ml (¼ pint, ⅝ cup US) double
  cream

1 tablespoon sour cream or cream
  or curd cheese
2 teaspoons French mustard
salt and freshly ground pepper
chives or parsley

Wipe and trim the mushrooms, but do not wash or peel them. Leave small ones whole, halve or quarter larger ones. Sprinkle with a little lemon juice.

Stir the cream with the sour cream or cheese until it is really thick (do not whip the cream as this makes it too light). Blend in the mustard, add enough lemon juice to give it some bite, season well and fold into the mushrooms, until they are well coated. Sprinkle with chopped chives or parsley.

French Bean Salad

SALADE D'HARICOTS VERTS

Strictly speaking, this salad should be made with the small, dark green French string beans, but it can also be made with runner beans, cut or broken into quite large chunks.

¾–1kg (1½– 2lb) French beans
sauce vinaigrette (see p. 51)

1 small onion or a few spring
  onions

Wash and string the beans if necessary, but leave them whole. Drop into a large pan of rapidly boiling salted water, bring the water back to a gentle boil and cook until just tender. This will take between 5 and 15 minutes, depending on the size and freshness of the beans. Be careful not to overcook, and do not cover the pan as they will lose some of their fresh green colour if you do. Drain as soon as they are cooked, rinse with cold water and spread out on a clean cloth to dry.

Place in a salad bowl or serving dish, sprinkle with the finely chopped onion, pour over the sauce vinaigrette and leave for at least ½ hour. Toss well before serving.

Tuna, Egg and Anchovy Salad

SALADE NICOISE

500g (1lb) French beans	*1 198g (7oz) tin tuna fish*
4 eggs	*4 or 5 tomatoes*
1 small lettuce	*1 50g (1¾oz) tin anchovy fillets*
70ml (⅛ pint, ¼ cup US)	*60g (2oz) black olives*
sauce vinaigrette (see p. 51)	

Top and tail the beans and cook them in boiling salted water for 5–15 minutes, or until they are just tender. Drain and cool. Hardboil the eggs.

Wash the lettuce, dry the leaves well and line a salad bowl with them. Dribble over a little of the vinaigrette. Flake the tuna fish roughly and make a mound in the centre of the bowl. Arrange the eggs, cut into quarters, and the tomatoes, also quartered, round the edge of the bowl, make a ring of the French beans round the tuna fish, and decorate the whole with the anchovy fillets and the olives. Dribble the remaining vinaigrette over the salad just before serving.

Tomato Salad

SALADE DE TOMATES

This should only be made in summer, with outdoor tomatoes full of the flavour of the sun.

450g (1lb) tomatoes
salt, preferably sea salt
freshly ground black pepper
1 tablespoon olive oil

2 shallots or 1 small onion
¼ clove garlic (optional)
small bunch parsley

Wash and slice the tomatoes, peeling them first if you wish. Season generously with salt and pepper, and sprinkle with the olive oil. Chop the shallots or onion, garlic and parsley together until quite fine, and sprinkle over the tomatoes.

Leave in a cool place for about ½ hour before serving.

Caper and Olive Dip

TAPENADE

Serve as a dip with plain biscuits or crudites (see p. 24) or mix with the yolks of hardboiled eggs to make stuffed eggs.

24 black olives, stoned (110g
    (4oz) weight before stoning)
2 tablespoons capers
8 fillets of anchovies

2 tablespoons olive oil
a good squeeze of lemon juice
freshly ground black pepper

Stone the olives and put them into a blender or mortar, together with the capers and anchovies, and blend or pound to a fine paste. Add the olive oil drop by drop, as you would for a mayonnaise. You should end up with a thick paste, much like a mayonnaise in consistency. Season to taste with the lemon juice and black pepper.

Pâtés and Terrines
•
Les Pâtés et Terrines

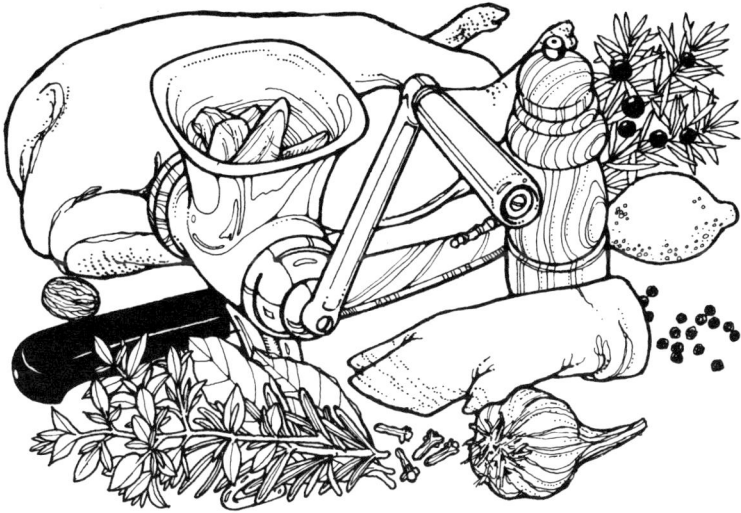

One of the prettiest sights in even the smallest French town
is the window of the charcuterie, artistically displaying the
local specialities. No other foods vary so widely from locality
to locality as sausages, rillettes, pâtés, terrines and galantines.

Though many imported pâtés can now be bought in
England, they tend to have a factory-made taste and texture.
It is not only a good deal cheaper to make your own, but the
result will be far more appetising.

Pâtés freeze extremely well, provided they have been well sealed, and are given at least 24 hours out of the freezer before serving, to allow the flavour to mature again.

There is no real difference between a pâté and a terrine. However, I have used the former term for the smooth spreadable sort of pâté, and terrine for the coarser, firmer product, which can be sliced for serving. It is an arbitrary distinction, but may help the reader to envisage the dish before making it.

Chicken Liver Pâté

PATE DE FOIE DE VOLAILLE

250g (8oz) chicken livers (or
    better still, a mixture of
    chicken and duck livers)
110g (4oz) butter
1 tablespoon brandy
1 tablespoon sherry

1 clove garlic
salt and freshly ground black
    pepper
pinch of mixed dried herbs
1 bayleaf

Pick over the chicken livers, removing any fatty gristle or greenish parts. If you are using frozen livers, they must be thoroughly thawed first.

Melt half the butter in a small frying pan and cook the livers gently and evenly for no more than 5 minutes – the livers should be brown on the outside and pink but not raw on the inside. Transfer the livers to a blender or Magimix. Add the brandy and sherry to the pan and bring quickly to the boil. Allow to bubble and reduce for one minute, then pour the contents of the pan into the blender. Add the peeled clove of garlic, plenty of salt and pepper, the dried herbs and the remaining butter and blend till smooth. If you do not have a blender or Magimix, mince or chop the livers to a fine purée before adding the remaining ingredients.

Pour into a small earthenware terrine, place the bayleaf on top and leave overnight in the refrigerator before serving, with thin toast or French bread.

If you wish to keep the pâté longer, melt a little more butter and pour it over the top of the terrine to seal the pâté. It will then keep for at least a week in the refrigerator or, well wrapped, for several months in the freezer.

Note : See also suggestion for serving at the end of Brioche recipe on p. 150.

Chicken and Lemon Terrine

TERRINE DE POULET AU CITRON

1 large roasting chicken (2kg, 4½lb approx.)
340g (12oz) belly of pork
250g (8oz) lean veal (from neck or shoulder)
2 eggs
2 tablespoons brandy

salt and freshly ground black pepper
pinch each of ground nutmeg, ground cloves and ground cinnamon
1 lemon
250g (8oz) sliced streaky bacon

With a sharp knife, cut along the ridge of the breastbone of the chicken, then pull the skin off the entire chicken. You will find it comes off like an overcoat. Keep the skin for making stock, together with the carcass and giblets. Cut the breast meat off in thick slices, and cut fillets of meat off the drumsticks and thighs, removing any inner skin and tendons. Set this meat aside. Cut the rest of the meat off the carcass.

Remove the skin and bones from the belly of pork. Mince the small pieces of chicken, the chicken liver, the belly of pork and the veal together, and put into a large bowl.

Beat the eggs with the brandy, plenty of salt and pepper and the spices, and blend this well into the minced meat. Fry a small pat of the mixture in a little butter to test for seasoning.

Cut the lemon into quarters lengthwise, and then cut out the flesh from between the inner divisions. Chop this roughly and blend into the meat mixture.

Remove the rind from the bacon and line a 1 litre (2 pint) terrine with some of the slices. Press in half the minced meat mixture, lay on the slices of meat, and cover with the remaining mixture. Lay any remaining bacon slices over the top.

Cover with a double layer of foil, stand in a bain-marie and cook in a moderate oven (180C, 350F, Mark 4) for 2½–3 hours. When cooked the pâté should have shrunk from the side of the dish and the juices should be clear.

Refrigerate overnight before serving.

Pork Liver Pâté

PATE DE FOIE DE PORC

*500g (1lb) bacon (back or
  streaky)
500g (1lb) pig's liver
2–3 cloves garlic
3–4 shallots or 1 medium onion
pinch of mace
pinch of ground cloves or nutmeg
3 tablespoons brandy*

*salt and freshly ground black
  pepper
small glass (70ml, ⅛ pint, ¼ cup
  US) white wine
2 carrots
1 onion
small bunch thyme and rosemary
1 bayleaf*

Remove the rind from the bacon and line a 1 litre (2 pint) terrine or other earthenware dish with some of the slices. Mince or chop finely the remaining bacon with the liver, the garlic and the shallots or onion. Mix well, add the spices and the brandy, and season liberally with the pepper, carefully with the salt, as the bacon may already have made the mixture sufficiently salty. Fry a small pat of the mixture in a little butter to test for seasoning.

Press the mixture into the lined terrine and pour over the white wine. Cover with the carrots cut into quarters lengthwise, the sliced onion and the bunch of herbs and bayleaf.

Cover the terrine tightly with foil, and a lid if possible, stand in a bain-marie and cook in a slow oven (160C, 325F, Mark 3) for 3½ hours.

Uncover the terrine, remove the vegetables and herbs, press the meat down well, and leave to cool. The juice should set to a clear light jelly that just covers the top of the terrine.

Leave for at least one day before serving.

Pork Terrine

TERRINE DE PORC

This has a coarser texture and more robust flavour than the pork liver pâté, and, thickly sliced, could well form the mainstay of a summer meal.

1¼kg (2½lb) belly of pork	1 egg
250g (½lb) pig's liver	2 tablespoons brandy
1 onion	salt and freshly ground black
2 cloves garlic	pepper
2 branches rosemary or	1 pig's trotter
2 teaspoons dried rosemary	

Skin and bone the belly of pork and mince together with the liver. Put in a large bowl. Chop the onion finely with the garlic and the leaves of one branch of rosemary. If you are using the dried herb, crumble it finely. Add to the meat. Beat the brandy into the egg, add to the bowl together with plenty of salt and pepper and blend all the ingredients well together. Fry a small pat of the mixture in a little butter to test for seasoning.

Spoon the mixture into a 1 litre (2 pint) earthenware or other ovenproof terrine. Press the pig's trotter, split into two, into the centre, together with the second branch of rosemary. Place in a bain-marie in a hot oven (220C, 425F, Mark 7) and after 15 minutes reduce heat to 190C (375F, Mark 5) and cook for a further 1–1½ hours, until the meat has shrunk away from the sides and the juice is clear.

Take out of the oven, remove the pig's trotter and the branch of rosemary and smooth over the top. Place a weight on top of the terrine and leave to cool.

Leave for at least one day before serving.

Pheasant Terrine

TERRINE DE FAISAN

1 pheasant	1 egg
30g (1oz) butter	pinch of mace
500g (1lb) lean veal (from neck	6 juniper berries
or shoulder)	½ teaspoon dried thyme
2 tablespoons brandy	salt and freshly ground black
2 tablespoons white wine or cider	pepper
225g (½lb) streaky bacon	3 bayleaves

Wipe the pheasant inside and out, rub it with salt and dot with the butter. Roast for 30 minutes in a hot oven (200C, 400F, Mark 6). Leave to cool.

Cut the veal into cubes and marinade for ½ hour in the brandy and wine.

When the pheasant is cool enough, carve the breast into thick slices and strip the rest of the meat off the bones. (The carcass may be used to make stock for soup.)

Remove the rind from the bacon and line a 1 litre (2 pint) terrine with some of the slices.

Mince or finely chop together the remaining bacon, the drained pieces of veal and the pheasant meat, leaving aside the sliced breast.

Beat the egg into the marinading liquid, add the mace, the crushed juniper berries, the thyme and the salt and pepper, and blend into the minced meat, together with the juices from the roasting pan. Fry a small pat of the mixture in a little butter to test for seasoning.

Press half the mixture into the lined terrine, lay on the slices of meat and top with the remaining mixture. Press in the bayleaves, cover with a sheet of buttered foil, stand the terrine in a bain-marie and cook in a low oven (140C, 275F, Mark 1) for 2 hours. When it is cooked, the pâté should have shrunk away from the sides of the dish. Leave to cool, then place in the refrigerator to set.

Leave the pâté for 24 hours before eating.

Soups • Les Potages

The French family's evening meal usually starts round a capacious tureen. Soup, mostly served hot even in summer, will always be freshly made, and often from very simple ingredients. The French excel at vegetable soups of all kinds, with the characteristic flavour of the particular vegetable being carefully preserved. Home-made stock will normally be used, and of course, when available, it makes the best soup; but stock cubes are a perfectly satisfactory substitute.

All the recipes in this section are for vegetable soups. Meat soups as such are uncommon in France, and I have included *Bouillabaisse* in the Fish section as, for most people, it is a meal in itself. With some regret, I decided to leave out the other famous kind of fish soup, the *Bisque*, whether made from lobster or crab or some other shellfish, because of the hideous cost of the raw materials.

Vegetable Soup

POTAGE BONNE FEMME

An old-fashioned and basic winter soup.

500g (1lb) potatoes	*1 litre (1¾ pints, 4⅜ cups US)*
3 large carrots	*water or stock*
2 large leeks	*salt and freshly ground black*
60g (2oz) butter	*pepper*
	parsley

Peel and dice the potatoes and carrots, and wash and slice the leeks finely, using most of the green parts.

Melt the butter in a large saucepan and add the carrots and leeks. Cover and cook gently for 10 minutes. Add the potatoes and stir well, so that they also become coated with the butter, then add the water or stock and boil rapidly for 10–15 minutes, until the vegetables are cooked. Season to taste.

You can serve the soup as it is, if you have diced the vegetables finely enough, or you can blend it or pass it through a nylon sieve or a mouli. Sprinkle with parsley before serving.

Carrot Soup

POTAGE CRECY

500g (1lb) carrots
1 large potato (225g, 8oz
    approx.)
1 small onion or shallot
60g (2oz) butter
2 teaspoons salt

1 teaspoon sugar
850ml (1½ pints, 3¾ cups US)
    chicken or veal stock
freshly ground black pepper
parsley

Peel the vegetables and chop them quite finely.

Melt the butter in a large saucepan, add the vegetables and the salt and sugar, cover and cook over a gentle heat for 15–20 minutes, until the carrots are quite soft. Add the stock, bring to the boil and simmer for a further 10–15 minutes, or until the carrots are completely tender. Blend, or pass the soup through a nylon sieve or mouli.

Return to the saucepan to heat through, taste for seasoning and add the pepper. Sprinkle with the finely chopped parsley before serving.

Watercress Soup

POTAGE DE CRESSON

2 good bunches watercress (110g,
    4oz minimum)
1 medium onion
30g (1oz) butter
30g (1oz) flour

850ml (1½ pints, 3¾ cups US)
    chicken or veal stock
salt and freshly ground black
    pepper
1 egg yolk
2 tablespoons double cream

Wash and pick over the watercress, and remove any very tough or hairy stalks. Peel and chop the onion.

Melt half the butter in a large, heavy saucepan and soften the onion. Add the watercress, cover and cook gently for 5 minutes. Sprinkle on the flour and cook for 5 minutes more, stirring well. Slowly blend in the stock, and leave to simmer for 5–10 minutes. Pass through a blender or mouli. Return to the saucepan, season to taste, and heat through well.

Stir the cream into the egg yolk, blend in a little of the soup, then pour this in a thin stream into the rest of the soup. Stir well and leave for a few minutes, off the heat, then stir in the remaining butter cut into small pieces. This will give the soup a rich, shiny look. Serve immediately.

Onion and Cheese Soup

SOUPE GRATINEE LYONNAISE

340g (12oz) onions	pinch of mixed herbs
100g (3½oz) butter	French bread
30g (1oz) flour	170g (6oz) gruyère or cheddar
1 litre (1¾ pints, 4⅜ cups US) water	cheese
salt and freshly ground black pepper	2 egg yolks
	1 tablespoon sherry or madeira

Peel and finely chop or mince the onions. Melt the butter in a large saucepan and cook the onions over a moderate heat for 5 minutes. Stir and do not allow to brown.

Sprinkle on the flour, stir and cook for a further 2 minutes. Add the water, season well and add the herbs. Bring to the boil, cover and simmer for 40 minutes, then blend the soup or put through a nylon sieve.

Slice the bread, allowing 2 thin slices per person, and dry in the oven or toast lightly. Line a heat-proof tureen with the slices, sprinkle on half the grated cheese, pour on the soup and sprinkle the remaining cheese over the top.

Put the tureen in the top of a hot oven (220C, 425F, Mark 7) and leave for 10–15 minutes until the cheese has melted and begins to form a golden crust.

Whisk the egg yolks with the sherry or madeira, pour into the soup and give the soup a really good stir. Serve very hot.

Onion Soup

SOUPE A L'OIGNON

500g (1lb) onions
60g (2oz) butter
1 tablespoon oil
½ teaspoon sugar
salt
1 tablespoon flour
1 litre (1¾ pints, 4⅜ cups US)
  beef stock

French bread
1 clove garlic
110g (4oz) cheddar or gruyère
  cheese
1–2 tablespoons brandy
  (optional)

Peel and slice the onions into fine rings. Melt the butter and oil in a large, heavy-bottomed saucepan, add the onions, cover and cook over a very gentle heat for 15–20 minutes until they are quite soft and creamy yellow. Take off the lid, sprinkle with the sugar and salt, raise the heat and cook, stirring frequently, for another 10–15 minutes, until the onions are a rich, deep golden brown. Sprinkle with the flour, and when this has browned, add the stock, stir well and simmer for 20–30 minutes. Test for seasoning.

Meanwhile, slice the bread thickly,. allowing one slice per person. Dry in a moderate oven or under a low grill until it is quite dried out and crisp. Rub each slice on both sides with the cut clove of garlic. Pile a little grated cheese on each slice, and melt under a hot grill until lightly browned.

Serve the soup, very hot, in individual bowls, floating one cheese crouton in each bowl. On a very cold day, or for special occasions, lace the soup with a little brandy before serving.

Leek and Potato Soup

POTAGE PARMENTIER

250g (½lb) potatoes
250g (½lb) leeks
30g (1oz) butter
1 litre (1¾ pints, 4¾ cups US)
    water or stock

salt and freshly ground black
    pepper
4 tablespoons cream
parsley

Peel and dice the potatoes, wash, trim and slice the leeks, including as much of the green parts as possible.

Melt the butter in a large heavy saucepan, and soften the vegetables. Add the water or stock, season well and simmer, uncovered, until the vegetables are tender. Pass through a blender or mouli. Return the soup to the pan and heat through. Season to taste.

Swirl in the cream and sprinkle with freshly chopped parsley just before serving.

Cream of Pea Soup

CREME DE PETITS POIS

Simplicity itself to make, and truly delicious when made with fresh young peas, but also excellent made with frozen peas.

500g (1lb) shelled peas, fresh or
    frozen (approx. 1kg (2¼lb)
    unshelled)
110g (4oz) butter
1 lettuce heart
1 teaspoon salt

1 teaspoon sugar
1 litre (1¾ pints, 4⅞ cups US)
    chicken or veal stock
140ml (¼ pint, ⅝ cup US) single
    cream

Melt the butter in a large saucepan and over a gentle heat add the roughly shredded lettuce. As soon as it begins to wilt, add the peas. If you are using frozen peas, raise the heat a little and cook, uncovered, until the peas have thawed. Then add the salt and sugar, cover and cook gently for 10 minutes. Add the stock, bring to the boil and simmer for a further 10–15 minutes, or until the peas are tender. Blend or pass through a nylon sieve or a mouli.

Return to the saucepan, taste for seasoning, heat through and serve with a swirl of cream in each bowl.

Tomato Soup

SOUPE DE TOMATES

1kg (2¼lbs) tomatoes	420ml (¾ pint, 1⅞ cups US) milk
1 small onion or shallot	280ml (½ pint, 1¼ cups US)
2 teaspoons salt	chicken or veal stock
1 teaspoon sugar	15g (½oz) butter
1 dessertspoon cornflour or	parsley
ground rice	

Cut the tomatoes up roughly and put them in a heavy saucepan with the finely chopped onion or shallot. Add the sugar and salt. Cover and cook gently for 10–15 minutes, or until the tomatoes are really soft.

Pass through a nylon sieve and return to the clean pan.

Make a smooth paste with the cornflour and a little milk and slowly stir this into the tomato purée over a gentle heat. Add the remaining milk, very slowly, taking care to keep the mixture smooth, bring to the boil and then add the stock. Simmer for 5 minutes. Season to taste and stir in the butter, cut into small dice.

Sprinkle with finely chopped parsley before serving.

Chilled Leek Soup

VICHYSSOISE

Though this beautiful summer soup can be made using stock cubes, it will be infinitely better made with real stock, especially if you can use a calf's foot or knuckle in the stock making, which will help to give the soup body.

1kg (2¼lb) leeks
250g (½lb) potatoes
30g (1oz) butter
1 litre (1¾ pints, 4⅜ cups US)
   chicken or veal stock

salt and white pepper
280ml (½ pint, 1¼ cups US)
   single cream
2 tablespoons chopped chives

Wash and chop the leeks, using only the white and very palest green parts. Peel and dice the potatoes.

Melt the butter in a large saucepan and soften the vegetables. Add the stock and a little seasoning and simmer until the vegetables are quite tender. Pass through a blender or mouli and leave to cool. Test for seasoning (the soup should be slightly oversalted at this point) and chill.

Just before serving, stir. in the cream, check seasoning and sprinkle with the chives.

Sauces • Les Sauces

'Good sauces are an indispensable part of good cooking. The more one knows about their preparation, the greater the variety in one's cooking. This does not mean that the sauces need be complicated or expensive. We shall show our readers how to master this art and thereby discover the secret of French cooking.' So says Tante Marie, who knew so well how to make all the processes of French cooking seem simple. There need be no mystique about the classic French sauces, and by grouping them together as I have done I hope to have shown how you can acquire a repertoire of sauces by developing variations on a few basic recipes.

Good sauces will always enhance, not mask, the dishes they are served with and, since they tend to be rather rich, should be served with moderation.

White Sauce

SAUCE BECHAMEL

30g (1oz) butter
30g (1oz) flour
420ml (¾ pint, 1⅞ cups US)
  milk or white stock

salt and white pepper
a knob of butter (optional)

Melt the butter in a heavy saucepan, blend in the flour and cook, without allowing to brown, over a gentle heat for 5 minutes. (The secret of making a fine-textured sauce lies in this thorough cooking of the flour.) Add the milk or stock bit by bit, stirring well and not adding more liquid until a smooth mixture has been obtained each time. When all the liquid has been absorbed, bring briefly to the boil and season to taste.

The sauce can be enriched by stirring in a knob of butter just before serving.

Variation

Cheese Sauce

SAUCE MORNAY

Béchamel sauce (see above)
60g (2oz) grated gruyére or
  cheddar cheese

1 egg yolk (optional)
1 tablespoon thick cream
  (optional)

Stir the cheese into the béchamel sauce and cook gently, stirring, until the cheese has melted. Remove from the heat and stir in the egg yolk and cream.

This sauce is particularly good with white fish (you can stir in a little of the fish cooking liquid), eggs and vegetables.

Hollandaise Sauce

SAUCE HOLLANDAISE

Delicious with eggs, fish, asparagus, artichokes or other delicate vegetables, and really not difficult to make.

3 egg yolks	*170g (6oz) butter*
1 tablespoon lemon juice	*salt and pepper*
1 tablespoon cold water	

Beat the egg yolks in a bowl together with the lemon juice and water, using a rotary or electric beater, until they are quite thick.

Place the bowl over a pan of barely simmering water. Cut the butter into small squares (about 1cm, ½in square). Add one cube of butter to the eggs at a time, and whisk or beat continuously, until the butter has melted and been absorbed. Do not add another piece of butter until the previous one has been amalgamated. This will take approximately 10 minutes of concentrated attention, but the method is virtually fool-proof. When all the butter has been absorbed, season to taste and serve.

The sauce may be kept warm for up to an hour, by setting the bowl in a pan of water kept just above lukewarm.

If by any chance the sauce should curdle, or refuse to thicken, start again in a clean warm bowl, with one tablespoon each of lemon juice and water, and slowly beat in the sauce, drop by drop at first, and then a little more quickly.

A quicker method of making this sauce, which is just as reliable, but produces a rather more bland sauce, is to use an electric blender. Blend the egg yolks with the lemon juice and water. Heat the butter in a saucepan until it is hot and just beginning to froth. Keeping the blender at full speed, add the butter drop by drop, until it has all been absorbed and the sauce has thickened.

Variations

Mousseline Sauce

SAUCE MOUSSELINE

Especially good with asparagus, artichokes or eggs. Fold
140ml (¼ pint, ⅝ cup US) of lightly whipped double or whipping cream, or crème fraîche, into the finished hollandaise,
just before serving.

Béarnaise Sauce

SAUCE BEARNAISE

Serve with fish, especially salmon or salmon trout, steaks or
chicken.

70ml (⅛ pint, ¼ cup US) wine vinegar (tarragon vinegar is especially good)	*1 shallot or small onion*
	strip of lemon peel
	salt and freshly ground black
70ml (⅛ pint, ¼ cup US) water	*pepper*
2 sprigs fresh tarragon if possible, otherwise 1 teaspoon dried	*3 egg yolks*
	170g (6oz) butter

Put the vinegar and water into a small saucepan, together
with the roughly chopped shallot or onion, the lemon peel,
the tarragon and a little salt and pepper, and boil fiercely for
about 5 minutes until reduced to about 2 tablespoons. Strain.
   Continue as for hollandaise, using this concentrated liquid
instead of lemon juice and water.

Mayonnaise

You can use any culinary oil to make mayonnaise, and the
finished product will vary accordingly. Olive oil makes the
heaviest and most richly flavoured mayonnaise, vegetable oil

the lightest. I usually find that a combination of half olive oil, half corn oil, gives very satisfactory results.

2 egg yolks	*salt and pepper*
1 tablespoon lemon juice	*280ml (½ pint, 1¼ cups US) oil*
1 teaspoon French mustard	

It is important that all ingredients and implements are at room temperature before you begin making mayonnaise. If the eggs have come out of the refrigerator, leave in warm water for a few minutes before separating.

Put the egg yolks in a bowl and beat with a wooden spoon or wire whisk. Add the lemon juice, mustard and salt and pepper and beat in. Begin to add the oil literally drop by drop, and beat well between each drop. Once you have added about 70ml (⅛ pint, ¼ cup US) of oil in this way, the sauce will have begun to thicken, and you can add the oil a little more quickly, but it should never be added in more than a very thin stream.

When all the oil has been absorbed, season the mayonnaise to taste, and add a little more lemon juice or a few drops of wine vinegar if it is too bland. If the sauce is too thick, beat in one or two tablespoons boiling water.

If the mayonnaise should curdle, there are several remedies. Start again in a clean bowl, either with another egg yolk, or a tablespoon of hot water, and beat in the curdled mayonnaise, a drop or two at a time, until you have a smooth sauce. Then add the rest of the mayonnaise a little more quickly.

You can also make mayonnaise in an electric mixer, blender or Magimix. This is certainly quicker, and as you can use the whole egg, more economical, but the finished product does not have quite the thick, glossy consistency of a handmade mayonnaise. Follow the instructions supplied with the appliance.

If the mayonnaise is to be used for covering cold meat, fish, eggs or vegetables for a cold table, add 1 teaspoon gelatine dissolved in a tablespoon of hot water, and fold in 140ml (¼ pint, ⅝ cup US) lightly whipped cream.

Variations

Rémoulade Sauce

SAUCE REMOULADE

Especially good with cold meat or fish. Fold in 2 tablespoons capers and gherkins, finely chopped, and 1 tablespoon finely chopped, mixed fresh herbs: parsley, chervil, tarragon, chives.

Green Mayonnaise

SAUCE VERTE

Very good for hors d'oeuvres, fish or meat. Boil a large handful of spinach or watercress with a little onion and parsley or tarragon. Drain very well, squeeze out all the moisture with your hands, then purée very finely and fold into the mayonnaise.

Garlic Mayonnaise

AIOLI

For garlic lovers, especially for hors d'oeuvres or fish and fish soup (see bouillabaisse, p. 54).

Start by mashing 3–4 (or more) cloves garlic very finely in a bowl, gradually add the egg yolks and beat them into the garlic. Then proceed as for basic mayonnaise.

Garlic, Pepper and Chilli Sauce

ROUILLE

For use with bouillabaisse (see p. 54) and crudités (see p. 24).
Also very good with cold meat, or blended into cream cheese.

1 red pepper	70ml (⅛ pint, ¼ cup US)
1 red chilli	olive oil
1 medium boiled potato	salt and pepper
4 cloves garlic	

Wash the pepper and chilli and remove the seeds. Blanch in
boiling water for 3 minutes.

Put the pepper, chilli, boiled potato and the peeled cloves
of garlic into a blender or mortar and blend to a smooth thick
paste. Add the olive oil drop by drop at first, then a little
faster, as for making mayonnaise, until you have a thick
smooth sauce. Season to taste.

French Dressing

SAUCE VINAIGRETTE

This is the standard French dressing for green salads. It may
be made with or without garlic, and the proportion of vinegar
to oil given here is approximate as vinegars and oils differ in
the amount of flavour and sharpness, so always taste a salad
dressing before adding to the salad. Olive oil makes the most
flavoursome dressing, but is very expensive, and so should
perhaps only be used for special occasions. At other times, a
mixture of olive and corn oil, or a corn or other good salad oil
may be used on its own.

The vinegar should always be a good wine vinegar, never
malt vinegar, which is much too sharp, and may be used alone
or with the addition of some lemon juice.

$\frac{1}{4}$ *clove of garlic (optional)* $\frac{1}{4}$ *teaspoon French mustard*
$\frac{1}{2}$ *teaspoon salt, preferably*   *1 teaspoon lemon juice (optional)*
    sea salt   *1 tablespoon wine sugar* or
plenty of freshly ground black $\frac{1}{2}$ *tablespoon vinegar and*
    pepper $\frac{1}{2}$ *tablespoon lemon juice*
$\frac{1}{4}$ *teaspoon sugar*   *3 tablespoons oil (see above)*

Crush the clove of garlic with the salt in the centre of the salad bowl if you like a fairly strong taste of garlic. If you like a hint of garlic only, rub the inside of the bowl lightly with the cut surface of the garlic clove. However, the garlic may be omitted altogether. Add the pepper, sugar and mustard, and mix to a smooth paste. Stir in the lemon juice and the vinegar, then add the oil slowly, stirring well the whole time so that it becomes amalgamated and forms a thick sauce.

Taste for seasoning. Add the lettuce just before serving and turn or toss it well so that all the leaves become coated. (Always be sure that lettuce leaves are quite dry before putting on the dressing, as the flavour will otherwise be sadly diluted.)

Variation

Vinaigrette Sauce with Herbs

SAUCE RAVIGOTTE

Very good served with cold meat or fish, or to make a salad with cold, cooked vegetables. Especially good served with cold globe artichokes (see p. 22).

1 teaspoon capers   *small bunch of chives*
2–3 shallots or *4–5 spring onions*   *140ml ($\frac{1}{4}$ pint, $\frac{5}{8}$ cup US)*
small bunch of parsley   *vinaigrette sauce*

Chop the capers, shallots, parsley and chives together to make a very fine hash. You should have $2\frac{1}{2}$–3 tablespoons of the mixture. Blend in the vinaigrette sauce.

Fish • Les Poissons

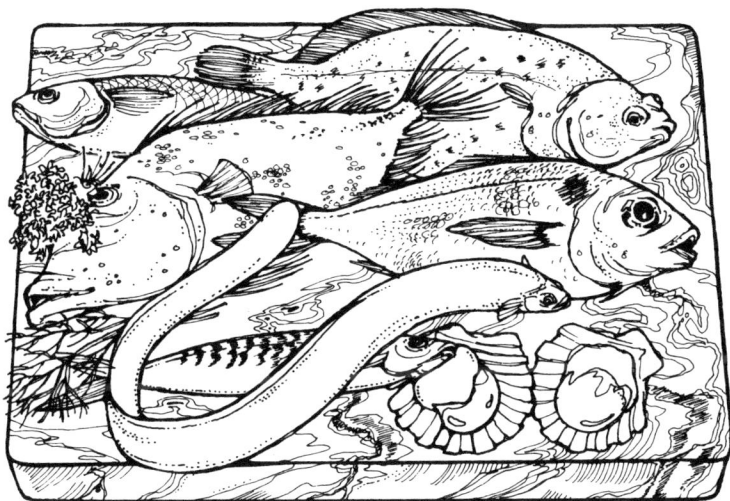

The French coastline is no longer than the coastline of the British Isles, but the French are more fortunate than we are in the far greater variety of fish regularly on sale in the French markets. North Sea and Atlantic fish come from the ports of Brittany, Normandy and the Pas de Calais, and many other species come ashore at Marseilles from the Mediterranean fishing grounds.

Many kinds of fish are delicious simply grilled with butter or oil, or lightly poached, but as the recipes that follow indicate, the French have devised a host of other ways of

serving fish that subtly enhance its individual flavour. All
these recipes use fish that is commonly available from most
British fishmongers.

Mediterranean Fish Soup

BOUILLABAISSE

A very good version of this richly flavoured speciality of
Marseilles, which is more of a meal than a soup, can be made
with fish that are available from most English fishmongers.
You can be as extravagant or as economical in your choice of
fish as you like, but the fish must be fresh or frozen whole –
the soup cannot be made from packets of frozen fish fillets.

Choose any 3 or 4 of the following – cod, eel, gurnard,
haddock, hake, halibut, John Dory, monkfish, sole, perch,
plaice, red or grey mullet, bream, snapper, trout, turbot.
Shellfish, such as lobster, or crab claws, add a luxurious
touch, but are not essential.

It is not worth making this dish in a small quantity, and the
following will feed 6–8 amply.

$1\frac{1}{2}$–2kg ($3\frac{1}{2}$–4lb) fish (3 or 4
  varieties, see above)
3 onions
1 carrot
sprig of fennel
2 bayleaves
small bunch of parsley
4 tablespoons olive oil
2 leeks
5 cloves garlic
2 tomatoes

1 tablespoon concentrated
  tomato purée
salt and freshly ground black
  pepper
a good pinch saffron
sprig of thyme or 1 teaspoon
  dried thyme
2 strips orange peel
30g (1oz) butter
dash of Pernod or anise
2 slices French bread per person

Clean, gut and scale the fish. It is particularly important to
scrape off all the scales, as these will otherwise spoil the soup,
but better not to skin the fish, so that the pieces will keep their
shape. Cut off the heads, tails and fins, put these in a large

saucepan together with 1 onion and the carrot, peeled and quartered, the sprig of fennel, the bayleaves and the stalks only of the parsley, cover with cold water (at least $2\frac{1}{4}$ litres, 4 pints, 10 cups US), bring slowly to the boil, skim and keep at a moderately fast simmer for 30 minutes.

Meanwhile cut the fish into thick slices; flat fish, such as plaice or sole, should be filleted, and the backbone added to the stock.

Melt 2 tablespoons of the oil in another large saucepan and soften the 2 remaining onions, the white parts of the leeks and 4 garlic cloves, all finely chopped. Do not allow to brown. Add the peeled chopped tomatoes and the tomato purée, then add the thick fish slices, turn well. Strain in the fish stock, add salt and pepper to taste, the saffron, thyme and orange peel, bring to the boil and boil gently for 10 minutes. Then add any filleted fish and shellfish, and keep at just above simmering point for a further 10 to 15 minutes, or until the fish is done.

Meanwhile rub the slices of French bread on both sides with the cut surface of the last garlic clove, dribble on a little olive oil and dry under a moderate grill. Just before serving, bring the soup to a rapid boil, add the last tablespoon of olive oil and the butter cut into small pieces. Finally add the dash of Pernod, and the finely chopped parsley.

Serve the soup in deep plates, with a round or two of the French bread floating in each. A bowl of rouille (see p. 50) or aioli (see p. 50) may be served separately so that those who wish to can add a dollop or two to their plates.

Creamed Salt Cod

BRANDADE DE MORUE

A speciality from the Languedoc area, but famous throughout France, and traditionally eaten on Fridays as a light lunch dish or first course for a richer meal.

500g (1lb) salt cod	*1 medium cooked potato*
3–4 cloves garlic	*(optional)*
140ml (¼ pint, ⅝ cup US) milk	*freshly ground black pepper*
140ml (¼ pint, ⅝ cup US) olive	*lemon juice*
oil	*fried bread or toast for serving*

Soak the salt cod in several changes of cold water for 24 hours.

Drain and rinse the cod and put in a large saucepan of cold water. Bring very slowly to the boil, and as soon as it begins to boil, remove saucepan from the heat. Cover and leave till cool enough to handle. Then drain, remove all skin and bones, and flake the fish.

Warm the milk and the oil very gently in separate saucepans.

Put the flaked fish and the crushed garlic cloves into a clean, large saucepan, and, using a wooden spoon over a very gentle heat, crush the fish and slowly work in the milk and oil, alternately, drop by drop, until they have all been absorbed and the brandade has the consistency of a thick cream. Season to taste with pepper and lemon juice.

If the brandade should curdle, work in a little warm mashed potato.

You can use an electric mixer, blender or Magimix to make the brandade, but the danger is that it will turn out too smooth and thin, so be careful not to overbeat.

Serve with warm triangles of fried bread or toast.

Scallops in the Shell

COQUILLES SAINT-JACQUES

English fishmongers, unlike the French, generally open and prepare scallops before selling them, leaving the meat attached to the flatter of the two shells. Ask for the deeper, top shell for this dish. Scallops can also be bought frozen, and these are quite good, though sometimes a little lacking in flavour. Use wide ramekin dishes if for any reason you do not have the shells.

Serve as a first course, or, if you wish to make a light supper dish, pipe some puréed potatoes round the edge to make it a little more substantial.

8 scallops (in the shell if possible)
140ml ($\frac{1}{4}$ pint, $\frac{5}{8}$ cup US) white wine
280ml ($\frac{1}{2}$ pint, $1\frac{1}{4}$ cup US) water
1 small onion
bouquet garni
strip of lemon peel
125g ($4\frac{1}{2}$oz) butter

125g (4oz) mushrooms
squeeze of lemon juice
30g (1oz) flour
1 egg yolk
2 tablespoons double cream
salt and pepper
1 tablespoon fine breadcrumbs
puréed potatoes (optional, see above)

Loosen the scallops from their shells, and wash well, discarding any inedible parts which may have been left – only the thick white muscle of the scallop and the crescent-shaped coral are edible. Scrub the top shells well on both sides.

Make a court-bouillon by boiling the wine and water with the onion, bouquet garni, lemon peel and a little salt for 5 minutes. Lower the heat, put the scallops in the pan and poach for 4–6 minutes, until just tender. Remove from the cooking liquor, slice thickly and set aside.

In a clean pan melt about 60g (2oz) of the butter and cook the finely sliced mushrooms with a squeeze of lemon juice until soft. Set aside and keep warm. In another pan, melt the remaining butter, keeping aside just 15g ($\frac{1}{2}$oz), add the flour and cook over a gentle heat for a few minutes. Slowly add the strained cooking liquor from the scallops and stir until smooth. Beat the cream into the egg yolk and stir into the sauce, being careful not to allow it to boil. Add the mushroom mixture and the scallops and heat through. Season to taste.

Divide the mixture evenly among the scallop shells or into the ramekin dishes. Sprinkle with the breadcrumbs and dot with the remaining butter. Add puréed potatoes if you wish (see above).

Brown quickly under a preheated grill and serve very hot.

Grilled Mullet

DAURADE GRILLEE

Mullet is a delicate and relatively bone-free fish, and lends itself particularly well to this simple Mediterranean way of cooking, which brings out the fresh fish flavour. Other fish, such as bream, snapper or mackerel, can also be cooked this way. If you can do the grilling over a charcoal fire, the aroma and flavour will be even more irresistible.

1 grey mullet (1kg, 2–2½lb for 4   1 lemon
   persons)   2–3 sprigs fresh rosemary
sea salt   1 tablespoon olive oil
freshly ground pepper

Wash the gutted fish well inside and out, scrape off the scales and, if you like, remove the head, tail and fins. Salt the inside well, and add a good sprinkling of pepper. Cut the lemon into quarters lengthways and, using one quarter, place a large piece of lemon peel and a sprig of rosemary inside, and add a squeeze of lemon juice. With a sharp carving knife, make deep diagonal incisions into both sides of the fish, at about 3cm (1½in) intervals. Sprinkle the first cooking side of the fish with more salt, pepper and lemon juice, dribble on half the olive oil and rub this in well. Place under the preheated grill, or over the charcoal grill when it has reached white heat, putting another sprig of rosemary over the top or underneath. When the first side is cooked, anoint the second side in the same way before cooking – a fish this size will take about 20 minutes on each side.

Serve with wedges of lemon, a salad and a bottle of chilled white wine.

Mackerel Stewed in Red Wine

MATELOTE DE MAQUEREAUX

The original matelote comes from Burgundy and is a stew of eels in Burgundy wine. However, the name may be used for any fish stew cooked in red wine, and this is a simple adaptation of the recipe for use with one of our best and most readily available fish, which, in its rich meatyness, is not too dissimilar to eel. It makes a very satisfying dish.

750g (1½lb) mackerel
1 large onion
1 large carrot
1 clove garlic
85g (3oz) butter

280ml (½ pint, 1¼ cups US) red wine
bouquet garni
salt and freshly ground black pepper
225g (½lb) button mushrooms

Gut the fish, wash well and cut into thick pieces.

Peel and slice the onion and the carrot, and finely chop the garlic. Melt 60g (2oz) of the butter in a flameproof casserole or heavy saucepan, add the vegetables, cover and cook for 5 minutes to soften without browning.

Lay the pieces of mackerel on top, add the wine, the bouquet garni and the seasoning, bring to the boil, then cover and lower the heat to just above simmering point, and cook for 15–20 minutes, until the fish is set and parts easily from the bones. The pieces of fish must not be allowed to disintegrate.

Lift out the fish with a slotted spoon and keep warm in a deep, heated serving dish. Add some of the onion and carrot.

Strain the cooking liquor into a saucepan, bring to the boil and boil for a few minutes to reduce. If necessary, thicken with a little beurre manié (see p. 20).

Meanwhile wash and trim the mushrooms and cook them very quickly over a high heat in the remaining butter. Scatter over the fish, pour on the cooking liquor and serve immediately.

Mussels Cooked in White Wine

MOULES MARINIERES

1kg (2lb) mussels	*1 onion*
bunch of parsley	*some sprigs of fennel (optional)*
280ml (½ pint, 1¼ cups US)	*bayleaf*
white wine	*freshly ground black pepper*

Scrub the mussels in a large basin of cold water, scraping off any seaweed or barnacles clinging to them, and pull off the 'beard'. Discard any mussels that are cracked or open. Place in a bucket or basin of fresh cold water and leave for at least an hour to allow the mussels to discharge their sand.

Chop all but a few stalks of the parsley finely.

Rinse the mussels under a running cold tap, then place in a very large saucepan together with the wine, the roughly chopped onion, the few remaining stalks of parsley and the bayleaf. Cover the saucepan and place over a very high heat for a few minutes only, shaking the pan from time to time. Take off the lid, and with a perforated spoon lift out any mussels that have opened and place them in a large, heated tureen. Continue until all the mussels have opened and been lifted out. The whole operation should not take more than 5 minutes or so.

Bring the liquid in the pan to a fast boil, then strain over the mussels in the tureen. Sprinkle with the chopped parsley and serve.

Serve in deep bowls or soup plates, and put some empty plates on the table for the discarded mussel shells. The French take each mussel out of its shell by using an empty shell in a pincer movement. You will quickly become efficient at this method. Place some finger bowls on the table, and soup spoons for the juice, for those who do not wish to use empty shells for drinking this.

The only proper accompaniment for this dish is some crisp French bread and a bottle of chilled white wine.

Variation

Mussels with Cream

MOULES A LA CREME

Moules Marinières	*½ teaspoon French mustard*
2 tablespoons double cream or	*1 lemon*
crème fraîche (see p. 16)	

Prepare the Moules Marinières as above.

Stir the mustard into the cream.

When the mussels have all been cooked and lifted out of the pan, strain the cooking juice into a clean saucepan, boil vigorously for a few minutes, then remove from the heat and stir in the mustard and cream. Pour this sauce over the mussels, sprinkle with the parsley and give each person a wedge of lemon in their bowl.

Skate with Black Butter

RAIE AU BEURRE NOIR

1kg (2lb) skate	*salt and pepper*
1 small onion	*2 tablespoons capers*
bouquet garni	*a handful of small parsley sprigs*
1 tablespoon vinegar (malt or	*170g (6oz) butter*
wine)	*3 tablespoons wine vinegar*

Wash the skate wings well under running water. Place in a large saucepan, cover with cold water, add the onion, the bouquet garni, the vinegar and plenty of salt and pepper, bring slowly to the boil, skim, then simmer for 15 minutes.

Lift the fish carefully out of the saucepan, drain and place in a preheated serving dish. Sprinkle with salt and freshly ground black pepper, and the roughly chopped capers. Keep hot.

Melt the butter in a small saucepan, and when sizzling hot put in the sprigs of parsley and fry till crisp and brown. Lift these out of the butter with a slotted spoon and sprinkle over the fish. Leave the butter on a high heat until it turns nut brown, then pour quickly over the fish before it begins to burn. Add the wine vinegar to the pan – it will bubble up and begin to evaporate almost immediately. Pour over the fish and serve at once, very hot.

Serve with plain boiled potatoes (called 'à l'Anglaise' in French!).

Fillets of Sole in White Wine Sauce

FILETS DE SOLE AU VIN BLANC

This is a rich and luxurious dish, and despite the number of processes, it does not take at all long to prepare. You may substitute plaice for the sole, which will make the dish more economical, and almost as good.

1kg (2lb) sole	sprig of tarragon
salt and white pepper	60g (2oz) butter
280ml ($\frac{1}{2}$ pint, $1\frac{1}{4}$ cups US) white wine	60g (2oz) flour
1 small onion	140ml ($\frac{1}{4}$ pint, $\frac{5}{8}$ cup US) thick double cream or crème fraîche (see p. 16)
1 tablespoon wine vinegar	
strip of lemon peel	1 tablespoon breadcrumbs

Fillet and skin the sole, or ask the fishmonger to do this for you. Keep all the bones and trimmings.

Wash and dry the fillets, season them lightly on both sides, roll up and lay them closely side by side in a buttered fireproof dish. Pour over the wine, cover with buttered paper and cook in a moderate oven (180C, 350F, Mark 4) for 15 minutes.

Meanwhile put the washed fish trimmings in a saucepan together with the onion, wine vinegar, lemon peel and tarragon, add just enough water to cover and boil fiercely, until almost all the liquid has evaporated. You will need only 140ml ($\frac{1}{4}$ pint, $\frac{5}{8}$ cup US) of concentrated fish stock.

In another saucepan, melt the butter, add the flour and cook over a low heat for 5 minutes. Stir well and do not allow to brown. Strain the fish stock and add 140ml ($\frac{1}{4}$ pint, $\frac{5}{8}$ cup US) to the roux, stirring well to make a smooth sauce. Stir in the cream (if it is not really thick, use rather more and boil it gently for 2–3 minutes, until it thickens).

Take the fish out of the oven when ready, pour the wine stock off into another saucepan and boil fiercely for 3 minutes to reduce. Keep the fish warm meanwhile.

When the wine has reduced, add slowly to the sauce and continue to stir over a gentle heat until you have a rich, thick, smooth sauce. Taste for seasoning, pour over the fish, sprinkle with the breadcrumbs and brown quickly under a hot grill.

Trout Fried in Butter

TRUITE A LA MEUNIERE

4 trout	1 tablespoon flour
1 tablespoon oil	85g (3oz) butter
salt and freshly ground black	$\frac{1}{2}$ lemon
pepper	some sprigs parsley

Gut the trout and wash well. (It is usual in France to leave on the heads.) Dry on kitchen paper. Season the olive oil with plenty of salt and pepper, then rub the trout with the oil and roll in the flour.

Heat 60g (2oz) of the butter in a frying pan, and when it is foaming hot put in the trout. Cook for about 5 minutes on each side, and take care that they do not stick on the bottom of the pan. When cooked, the fish should have a thin, golden crust.

Remove the fish to a heated serving plate, add the sprigs of parsley to the pan and brown them quickly. Cut the lemon into 5 wedges, and add the juice of one of the wedges and the remaining butter, cut into small pieces, to the frying pan. As soon as this begins to foam, pour over the trout, place a lemon wedge on each fish and serve at once.

Variation

Trout with Almonds

TRUITE AUX AMANDES

Add 30g (1oz) flaked almonds to the pan instead of the sprigs of parsley, and fry them golden brown before completing the dish as above.

Meat • Les Viandes

A French butcher regards his craft as akin to art, and will cut and present the cheaper cuts of meat with as much care as the prime joints, just as the housewife will take as much trouble to make an appetising daube or blanquette for every day with the less choice parts of beef or veal, as she will take over a rôti or gigot for special occasions. I have therefore included recipes for both kinds of dish, and have given the nearest English equivalents to French joints, since these are cut rather differently from ours.

You will not find many pork recipes here, as pork in France is used chiefly for making sausages and other charcuteries.

Beef and lamb are invariably cooked for shorter periods and eaten 'rare' or 'medium rare'. Even if this is not what you are used to doing, please try it, especially with lamb – you may find it quite a revelation.

Beef Braised in Wine

BOEUF A LA MODE

This dish is equally good eaten hot or cold. Served cold it looks very pretty and is ideal for a buffet party, as the sauce sets into a beautiful clear, light jelly. For this, it must be made a day ahead.

2–2½kg (4–5lb) piece beef, topside, silverside or rump, boned and rolled '

110g (4oz) bacon or pork fat for larding (see below)

1 clove garlic

salt and freshly ground black pepper

2 teaspoons dried mixed herbs

60g (2oz) butter or chicken fat

2 onions

2 carrots

2–4 tablespoons brandy

280ml (½ pint, 1¼ cups US) red or white wine

approx. 1 litre (1½–2 pints, 3¾–5 cups US) water or stock

bouquet garni

1 strip orange peel

2 whole cloves

1 calf's foot or 2 pig's trotters, split

1kg (2lb) carrots

As the meat will be cooking for a long time, it is important that it should not become dry, and for this reason there must be sufficient fat content. Topside is usually prepared by English butchers with a sheet of fat tied round it, but you may need to lard – that is, to introduce thin strips of pork or bacon fat into the meat with a larding needle – other joints. Many butchers will be glad to do this for you.

Rub the meat all over with the cut surface of the clove of garlic, then rub in plenty of salt and pepper and the dried herbs.

Heat the butter or fat in a flameproof casserole which will

comfortably hold the meat, and brown it quickly on all sides. Add the sliced onions and the two carrots and brown these also. Pour in the brandy, let it bubble fiercely for a minute, then add the wine and bring to the boil. Add enough stock or water to come just to the top of the meat. Add the bouquet garni, orange peel and cloves.

Meanwhile place the calf's foot or trotters in a saucepan, cover with cold water and bring quickly to the boil. Allow to boil for 2 minutes, then pour off the water and rinse well in cold water. Add to the casserole.

Seal the casserole with a double layer of foil under the lid, then place in a slow oven (150C, 300F, Mark 2), or leave to simmer extremely slowly on top of the stove, for 2–4 hours, depending on the size and quality of the meat.

Meanwhile peel or scrape the carrots. Leave new carrots whole and cut older ones lengthwise into halves or quarters. Boil in salted water until just tender.

For Serving Hot

When the meat is cooked, lift out, slice thickly and keep warm on a deep serving dish. Strain the sauce into a bowl, skim off as much fat as possible. Arrange the cooked carrots around the meat, pour over the sauce and serve.

For Serving Cold the Following Day

Lift out the meat and strain the sauce into a bowl. Refrigerate for 4–5 hours, or overnight. Then lift off the lid of fat which will have formed on top, and scrape off the top layer of rather cloudy jelly which will have set just underneath the fat. Melt down the remaining jelly over a gentle heat. Slice the meat thickly and arrange on a deep serving platter, surrounded by the freshly cooked carrots. Pour over the sauce and refrigerate for 4–5 hours before serving.

Casserole of Beef with Burgundy

BOEUF BOURGUIGNON

1–1½kg (2½–3lb) best chuck steak
  or topside
60g (2oz) flour
salt and freshly ground black
  pepper
140g (5oz) butter
3 tablespoons olive oil
2 tablespoons brandy (optional)
½–¾ bottle red Burgundy wine

some beef stock, optional, see
  recipe
110g (4oz) green streaky bacon
2 onions
2 carrots
1–2 cloves garlic
500g (1lb) small onions or
  shallots
500g (1lb) button mushrooms

Cut the beef into large cubes, removing any fat or gristle. Season the flour very liberally with the salt and pepper, and roll the beef cubes in it, a few at a time, so that they each become thinly coated in the flour. Heat half the butter with the olive oil in a heavy frying pan, and when quite hot fry the beef cubes quickly until they are golden brown on all sides. Remove each batch as it is ready and put in a large earthenware or flameproof casserole. When all the meat has been fried, pour the brandy into the frying pan, and as soon as it begins to evaporate pour in the red wine. Stir well to remove any sediment from the pan, and when the wine begins to bubble, pour it over the meat in the casserole.

The liquid should just come level with the meat, and, if you do not want to use so much wine, you can make it up with a little beef stock.

Cut the bacon into thin strips and fry gently using a little of the remaining butter. Chop the onions, carrots and garlic together till quite fine and fry with the bacon until everything just begins to brown. Add to the casserole.

Place the casserole in a slow oven (150C, 300F, Mark 2) or on top of the stove over a very low heat, and cook gently until the meat is tender. This will take between 2 and 3 hours, depending on the quality of the meat.

After one hour, brown the small onions or shallots in half the remaining butter and add to the casserole.

Just before serving, cook the button mushrooms quickly in the remaining butter, without a lid, so that some of the moisture evaporates, and add to the casserole.

Casserole of Beef with Olives

BOEUF EN DAUBE PROVENCALE

A daube is one of those age-old French household recipes, for which exact ingredients, proportions and methods will vary from cook to cook. The vital characteristic of a daube is that the meat is cooked very, very slowly with wine and herbs in a well sealed casserole and, though a gentle aroma will steal out and fill the house, when the lid is finally lifted off the casserole, the smell will be irresistible.

The long, slow cooking will transform even the cheapest cuts, so though for special occasions top side or rump steak may be used, chuck steak or even best quality stewing steak will make an excellent dish, as far removed from the ordinary stew as it is possible to be. The daube provençale is distinguished from other daubes by the addition of olives, but these may be omitted if preferred.

1kg (2lb) beef (see above)	*thyme, parsley, bayleaf*
170g (6oz) salt pork or streaky bacon	*strip of orange peel*
2 onions	*salt and freshly ground black pepper*
2 carrots	*420ml ($\frac{3}{4}$ pint, $1\frac{7}{8}$ cups US) red wine*
2 cloves garlic	
3 tomatoes	*12 black olives*
1 tablespoon olive oil	

Trim the meat. Top side should be left in one piece, rump steak may be left in a piece or cut into thick slices, chuck or stewing steak should be cut into substantial squares, with any fat or gristle removed.

Cut the rind off the bacon or salt pork, and cut both rind and bacon or pork into small squares. Peel and scrape onions, carrots and garlic and slice fairly thinly. Skin the tomatoes and chop roughly.

Heat the oil in a flameproof casserole just large enough to hold all the ingredients. Put in the pieces of bacon or pork and rind, and fry quickly until transparent. Add the vegetables and soften. Place the meat on top, add the herbs and orange peel and seasoning, and cook over a moderate heat without covering for about 10 minutes, until the meat begins to colour.

Bring the wine to the boil in a separate saucepan and boil fast for 5 minutes to reduce. Pour over the meat – the liquid should just be level with the top of the meat. Place a piece of foil or greaseproof paper over the top of the casserole, put on the lid and place in a very slow oven (140C, 275F, Mark 1) and cook for anything from 3–5 hours, depending on the quality of the meat. The meat should be completely tender, and the sauce reduced almost to the consistency of jam.

Add the stoned olives to the casserole half an hour before serving time. Serve with baked potatoes or noodles, or simply with a green salad.

Beef Braised in Beer

CARBONNADE DE BOEUF FLAMANDE

1kg (2–2¼lb) braising beef)
  (chuck or skirt are very
  suitable)
salt and freshly ground black
  pepper
500g (1lb) onions
60g (2oz) butter or good beef
  dripping

1 tablespoon oil
30g (1oz) flour
1 teaspoon brown sugar
1 tablespoon red wine vinegar
½ litre (good ¾ pint, 1⅞ cups US)
  dark ale or stout (or use half
  beer and half stock)
bouquet garni

Trim any fat or gristle off the meat and cut into large cubes. Season well with the salt and pepper. Peel the onions and cut into moderately fine rings.

Heat the butter or dripping with the oil in a flameproof casserole, and when smoking hot fry the beef cubes till browned on all sides. Do not put in more than can lie on the bottom of the casserole at any one time. Take out each batch as it browns and set aside.

Lower the heat a little and fry the onions in the casserole till soft and gold, but not brown. Remove from the casserole and set aside.

Sprinkle the flour into the casserole and cook over a moderate heat, stirring well, until it is dark golden. Add the sugar and the vinegar, and when the vinegar has evaporated, slowly add the beer, stirring well to scrape up any sediment from the bottom.

Layer the meat and onions in the casserole, add the bouquet garni, cover, bring to the boil and then cook in a slow oven (150C, 300F, Mark 2), or simmer over a very low flame, for 2–3 hours, until the meat is very tender and the sauce has thickened.

Remove the bouquet garni, skim off any excess fat from the top of the casserole, test for seasoning and serve hot, with noodles or baked potatoes.

Fillet of Beef in Pastry Case

FILET DE BOEUF EN CROUTE

1kg (2lb approx.) fillet of beef	*1 Spanish onion*
salt and freshly ground black	*110g (4oz) mushrooms*
pepper	*1 tablespoon brandy*
1 clove garlic	*370g (13oz) puff pastry*
60g (2oz) butter	*1 egg yolk*

Rub the fillet all over with salt and pepper and the cut surface of the clove of garlic.

Melt the butter in a frying pan and gently brown the meat in it on all sides. Take the meat out of the pan and set aside to cool.

Chop the onion and mushrooms together to make a fine hash, add to the butter in the pan and cook until soft. Pour on the brandy, raise the heat and let the mixture bubble until it is quite thick. Pour on to a plate to cool.

Roll out the pastry to form 2 unequal rectangles. Lay the smaller in a roasting tin, lined with buttered foil. Put half the cooled mushroom mixture in the centre and the fillet on top, and cover with the remaining mushroom mixture. Place the larger rectangle of pastry carefully over the top and make a neat parcel, sealing the edges well. Use any left-over pastry to decorate the top.

Beat the egg yolk with a little water and brush the pastry with it. Place in a hot oven (220C, 425F, Mark 7) for 20 minutes, lower the heat to 190C (375F, Mark 5) and cook for a further 10–15 minutes, not more. The pastry should be golden brown and risen on top, and the meat inside just cooked 'à point' – that is, pale brown on the outside and pink in the centre.

Beef Olives

PAUPIETTES DE BOEUF

A good way of stretching one of the more expensive cuts of beef. This quantity will feed 6.

½–¾kg (1–1½lb) topside of beef or rumpsteak	1 egg
	1 tablespoon flour
110g (4oz) bacon	280ml (½ pint, 1¼ cups US) stock (approx.)
2 onions	
110g (4oz) mushrooms	1 small clove garlic
60g (2oz) breadcrumbs	1 tablespoon French mustard
strip of lemon peel	salt and freshly ground black pepper
large handful parsley	

Cut the meat into thin slices and cut off any fat. Beat the slices till very thin and trim into fairly even shapes.

Take the rinds off the bacon and cut off the fat.

Melt the pieces of beef and bacon fat gently in a flameproof casserole, then remove the pieces when the fat has run from them.

Chop the onions, parsley, lemon peel, mushrooms, bacon and trimmings of beef together until you have a very fine hash. Mix in the breadcrumbs and bind the mixture with the lightly beaten egg. Season with a little pepper – it should be salty enough from the bacon.

Place a spoonful of this mixture on to each slice of meat, roll up into a sausage shape and either tie with some cotton or thin string, or secure with sausage sticks.

Quickly brown the beef olives in the fat in the casserole, then remove to a plate. Sprinkle the flour into the casserole, cook, stirring well, till lightly browned, then add the stock and stir to make a smooth sauce. Add the crushed clove of garlic. Return the beef olives, cover and simmer for 35–45 minutes until tender. Stir the mustard into the sauce, and test for seasoning before serving.

Boiled Beef

POT AU FEU

A traditional French recipe, which may sound complicated but is really very simple to make, and highly economical, providing several meals from one cooking session. There are no hard and fast rules about the cut of beef to be used, except that the larger the piece the better (anything less than 1 kg (2¼lb) is not worth using) and that some bones should be included. Top rib, silverside, brisket or forequarter flank all give excellent results, and the addition of a knuckle of veal or a beef marrow bone, or preferably both, add body to the broth. A chicken carcass, chicken giblets or even a boiling fowl are sometimes added for good measure. The only other essential is a really large cooking pot.

2¼–2½kg (4–5lb) piece of beef
(see above)
knuckle of veal (see above)
beef marrow bone (see above)
water
4 onions
675g (1½lb) leeks
675g (1½lb) carrots
2 tomatoes

stick of celery
bouquet garni
salt

For Serving
some rounds of French bread
a dash of white wine, vermouth
* or sherry (optional)*

Make sure the meat is securely tied so that it does not fall apart in the long, slow cooking. If you are using a marrow bone, tie it up in muslin to keep in the marrow.

Put the meat, knuckle of veal, and any chicken bones (see above) into your largest pot, add 4½ litres (8 pints, 20 cups US) of water, or as much as your pot will hold if it is not quite large enough. (There should, if possible, be about 1 litre (1¾ pints, 4⅜ cups US) of water to each half kg of meat.) Bring very slowly to the boil and for the next half hour skim off all the scum that will rise to the top. When no more grey scum appears, put in the onions, washed but not peeled, 2 large leeks, washed but left whole, 3 or 4 scraped carrots, and the tomatoes, which have been halved and lightly grilled. Add the stick of celery, the bouquet garni and about 1 tablespoon of cooking salt. Cover and leave to simmer very, very gently for about $3\frac{1}{2}$ hours, then add the marrow bone and cook for another hour.

The dish is now ready to serve, in two parts: as a clear consommé (or bouillon) to start with, to be followed by the boiled beef, the bouilli, with the remaining carrots, leeks and some boiled potatoes. These vegetables can be added to the pot to be cooked in the broth for the last half hour, but are actually rather nicer if cooked separately.

Lift out the beef and keep warm until ready to serve. If a marrow bone has been used, lift out carefully and set aside for the moment.

Strain the broth through a large sieve, and then strain again through a damp muslin cloth or a double thickness of kitchen paper laid in the strainer. Skim off any fat, first with a spoon, then by briefly laying absorbent kitchen paper over the top, and removing it as soon as it has become saturated. There will probably be more broth than needed for one meal, so taste for seasoning and season only the amount to be served at this meal. If a marrow bone has been used, take out the marrow, spread on pieces of toasted or baked bread and serve with the broth. A dash of white wine, vermouth or sherry added to the broth is an optional improvement.

The remaining broth can be used to make soups at other times, and can be kept in the refrigerator for 3 or 4 days, or much longer in the freezer. If the stock is to be frozen it is best to leave it in the refrigerator overnight to allow any fat to rise to the top and set. Lift off the fat and boil rapidly until much reduced. Cool and freeze as concentrated stock.

Any left over beef can be served cold the next day. It is particularly good served with an aioli (see p. 50) or a sauce ravigotte (see p. 52). Or make a salade de boeuf (see next recipe).

Cold Beef Salad

SALADE DE BOEUF

1kg (2lb) potatoes
450g (1lb) cold boiled or roast
   beef
2 hardboiled eggs

140ml (¼ pint, ⅝ cup US) sauce
   ravigotte (see p. 52)
parsley

Boil the potatoes in their skins until they are just cooked. Drain, and as soon as they are cool enough to handle, peel and slice them thinly.

Cut the beef into thin slices, and then into strips about 1cm (½in) wide. Put a layer of the potatoes, which should still be warm in a shallow dish, anoint them generously with the sauce ravigotte, put a layer of beef on top, dribble on a little of the sauce, and repeat until the ingredients have been used, finishing with potatoes and the sauce.

Garnish with the finely chopped hardboiled eggs and some chopped parsley.

Peppered Steaks

STEAK AU POIVRE

4 steaks, 1 per person (225–340g,
   8–12oz each)
1 tablespoon peppercorns, black,
   or a mixture of black and
   white
1 small onion

60g (2oz) butter
½ tablespoon oil
salt
140ml (¼ pint, ⅝ cup US) stock
   or water
3 tablespoons brandy

Trim the steaks, cutting off excess fat, and make small incisions round the edges where there is fat or gristle, to prevent the steaks from curling when cooking. Dry them well on kitchen paper.

In a pestle and mortar, or using a broad-bladed knife and wooden board, crush the pepper corns. (Do not put them through a grinder, which makes them too fine.) Sprinkle both sides of each steak with the crushed pepper, and press it well in. Leave for at least half-an-hour for the pepper taste to permeate the steaks.

Chop the onion very finely.

Heat half the butter with the oil in a frying pan over a high heat. When it is smoking hot, but not burning, lower the heat a little, put in the steaks and cook them for 3–5 minutes on each side, depending on how thick they are and how rare you like them. When they are cooked to your satisfaction, remove the steaks to a heated platter, sprinkle with salt and keep warm. Add the onion to the pan and cook until soft, then add stock or water and bring to a rapid boil. Stir well to scrape up any sediment from the pan, and boil for 3–4 minutes to reduce. Add the brandy and continue to boil hard for another 2 minutes, to evaporate the alcohol.

Cut the remaining butter into small pieces, add these to the pan and swirl it round till the butter melts. This will thicken and glaze the sauce. Pour quickly over the steaks and serve at once.

The best accompaniment is a watercress or other green salad.

Lamb Baked with Potatoes and Aubergines

CARBONNADE NIMOISE

An economical dish which will feed 6 people generously. The exact proportions of vegetables to the meat, or to each other, are not important, and the dish can easily be stretched to feed more by increasing the amount of vegetables.

English butchers sometimes sell slices of leg of lamb, or lamb steaks, and these are ideal for this dish. However, you can make your own by boning a leg of lamb, or asking the butcher to do this for you, and then cutting the meat into thick slices. (Remember that no French housewife would discard the bone of the leg, but would make a good stock or bouillon from it, using plenty of herbs, especially marjoram, to flavour it.)

1–1¼kg (2–2½lb) sliced leg of
lamb or
1 leg of lamb (1½–2½kg, 3–5lb)
1kg (2lb) aubergine (or more)
2–3 cloves garlic
1kg (2lb) potatoes (or more)

110g (4oz) bacon
2 tablespoons olive oil
salt and freshly ground black
pepper
1 teaspoon dried herbs (thyme,
marjoram, rosemary)

Wash, but do not peel the aubergines, cut into small squares approximately 1cm (½in) square. Sprinkle liberally with salt and leave for at least 1 hour in a colander to drain.

Prepare the meat as above, spike each piece with a sliver or two of garlic, and sprinkle with salt and pepper. Peel and dice the potatoes. Cut the bacon into strips.

Heat the oil in a large roasting tin or flat baking dish. Scatter the bacon over the bottom, add the slices of lamb and then the potatoes and the rinsed and dried aubergines. Sprinkle with salt, pepper and herbs, and put in a hot oven (230C, 450F, Mark 8). After 20 minutes, lower the oven temperature to 180C (350F, Mark 4). Cover the dish with a lid or a double thickness of foil, sealed round the edges, and cook for a further 2–3 hours, until the meat and vegetables are very tender and most of the liquid has been absorbed.

Casserole of Beans with Lamb and Pork

CASSOULET

An age-old country dish for the winter months, when fresh meat and vegetables are scarce and stomachs need lining against the cold. Recipes for cassoulet vary from region to region in France, one of the best known being the Cassoulet de Toulouse, which includes pieces of the preserved goose (confit d'oie) for which the region is famous. But a perfectly good cassoulet can be made without these, and this rich, satisfying dish is well worth the rather prolonged preparation and cooking time. A really large cassoulet pot, or casserole, preferably earthenware, is vital. If you do not have one large enough to hold these ingredients, you will need to bone and cube the meat first, but there is little point in making the dish

in smaller quantities than these, which will serve 10–12 people
generously.

1kg (2lb) white haricot beans	*4 tablespoons concentrated*
250g (8oz) salt pork or bacon in	*tomato purée*
one piece	*500g (1lb) uncooked garlic*
500g (1lb) loin of pork	*sausage (whole)*
2 tablespoons oil or dripping	*salt and freshly ground black*
2 onions	*pepper*
3 cloves garlic	*bouquet garni*
1 small shoulder of lamb (or ½	*110g (4oz) fresh breadcrumbs*
large)	*(or more, see recipe)*

Rinse the beans under cold running water, then put in a large
saucepan with as much cold water as it will hold, cover and
bring to the boil. Simmer for 5 minutes, then remove from
the heat and leave, covered, for about 40 minutes.

Meanwhile, remove the rind as thinly as possible from the
salt pork or bacon and from the loin of pork, and cut it into
small squares.

Heat the oil or dripping in a large drying pan and soften
the finely sliced onions and garlic. Add the pieces of rind and
cook for 5 minutes. Raise the heat and quickly brown first the
piece of pork and then the shoulder of lamb on all sides.
Remove these from the frying pan and stir the tomato purée
into the remaining ingredients in the pan.

When the beans are ready, drain them, rinse the saucepan
and return the beans with 1¾ litres (3 pints, 7½ cups US) of cold
water. Bring to the boil, then pour into the cassoulet pot. Bury
the pieces of bacon, pork and lamb and the garlic sausage
in the beans, and pour on the contents of the frying pan.
Season well and add the bouquet garni. Bring to simmering
point on top of the stove, then sprinkle a thick layer of breadcrumbs on top and place in a low oven (150C, 300F, Mark 2)
and cook for 3–4 hours. From time to time, press the crust of
breadcrumbs that will have formed on top down with the back
of a spoon and sprinkle on a further layer of crumbs. Add a
little water to the casserole if it seems to be getting too dry.

Before serving, take out the pieces of pork and lamb and
the sausage and cut into convenient chunks.

Shoulder of Lamb with Baked Potatoes

EPAULE D'AGNEAU BOULANGERE

1 shoulder of lamb (see also note
  below)
1 clove garlic
1kg (2lb) potatoes (preferably
  the floury, King Edward
  variety)

2 large onions
280ml ($\frac{1}{2}$ pint, 1$\frac{1}{4}$ cups US)
  stock or water
salt and freshly ground pepper
15g ($\frac{1}{2}$oz) butter
parsley

Rub the shoulder all over with the cut surface of the clove of garlic, salt and pepper.

Peel the potatoes and cut them across into slices $\frac{1}{4}$cm (good $\frac{1}{8}$in) thick. Rinse well in cold water to extract some of the starch. Peel the onions and cut them into thin rings.

Butter a roasting tin or a large, shallow ovenproof dish. Place the potato slices, interspersed with the onion rings, in an even layer on the bottom, sprinkle with salt and pepper, place a rack over the top and put on it the shoulder of lamb. Pour the boiling stock or water over the potatoes, dot the meat with the remaining butter and bake in a moderately hot oven (190C, 375F, Mark 5) for 1$\frac{1}{2}$ hours, or until the meat is cooked, but still pink, so that when a skewer is inserted into it, a clear light pink liquid runs out.

Turn the potatoes once or twice during the cooking time. They should at the end be quite soft and delicately flavoured by the stock and meat juices which they will have absorbed. Sprinkle them with the finely chopped parsley.

Carve the meat, and serve separately, or place the slices on top of the potatoes before serving.

Note: For a very economical version of this dish, use neck of lamb, chops or breast of lamb instead of the shoulder. They will need about $\frac{1}{2}$ hour less cooking time and the potatoes should therefore be pre-boiled for 5 minutes first.

Leg of Lamb with Haricot Beans

GIGOT D'AGNEAU AUX HARICOTS

500g (1lb) haricot beans	1 tin (396g, 14oz) Italian
3 onions	peeled tomatoes
1 carrot	parsley
bayleaf	1 leg of lamb (1½–2½kg, 3–5lb)
2 sprigs of thyme or 1 teaspoon	1 oz butter
dried thyme	280ml (½ pint, 1¼ cups US)
1 tablespoon olive oil	water
3 cloves garlic	salt and freshly ground black
	pepper

Rinse the beans under cold running water, then put in a large saucepan with as much cold water as it will hold, cover and bring to the boil. Simmer for 5 minutes, then remove from the heat and leave, covered, for about 40 minutes. Then drain and rinse the beans, put back in the clean saucepan and cover plentifully with cold water. Bring very slowly to the boil, skim, add one onion and the carrot, peeled and quartered, the bayleaf and thyme, then simmer until the beans are just tender to the bite. This may take anything from 1–3 hours, depending on how fresh they are. Remove from the heat and drain well. Discard the onion, carrot and herbs.

In a flameproof casserole, preferably one in which the finished dish can be brought to table, heat the oil and gently fry the remaining onions and one clove of garlic, all finely chopped, until they are soft. Add the drained beans, turn well, add the tinned tomatoes and a little more thyme, cover and leave to simmer until the beans are quite tender, but not broken or mushy. Season to taste (if you add salt sooner the beans may become tough) and stir in the finely chopped parsley just before serving.

The beans may be prepared ahead of time, and reheated shortly before the meal.

About 1½ hours before the meal is to be served, cut the remaining cloves of garlic into thin slivers, make incisions near the bone of the leg of lamb, and in its skin all around, and insert the slivers of garlic. Rub the leg with salt and brush all over with the melted butter. Place on a rack in a roasting tin, pour the water into the tin and roast the lamb in a moderately hot oven (190C, 375F, Mark 5), basting fairly frequently. Allow 40 minutes to the kilo, 20 minutes to the pound. When cooked the meat should be tender and, if a skewer is inserted right to the bone, a thin pink juice should run out.

Carve the meat into thick slices – it should be pale pink, neither raw and bloody, nor grey or brown. Pour the juice from the roasting pan and the carving board over the beans, and lay the slices of lamb on top. Serve.

Alternatively, the dish may be served on a large heated platter, with the slices of meat in the centre, surrounded by the beans.

Note : You can also use a shoulder instead of a leg of lamb for this recipe.

Marinated Roast Leg of Lamb

GIGOT MARINE

This method of cooking lamb gives it a full-bodied, somewhat gamey, flavour.

1 leg of lamb (1½–2½kg, 3–5lb)	*1 small onion*
140ml (¼ pint, ⅝ cup US) olive oil	*2 bayleaves*
	strip of lemon peel
2 tablespoons wine vinegar	*salt and freshly ground black pepper*
3–4 cloves garlic	
large sprig each thyme, rosemary and marjoram or	*30g (1oz) butter*
1 teaspoon each dried herbs	*water*

Measure the oil and vinegar into a shallow dish, add the lightly crushed garlic cloves, the roughly chopped onion, the herbs, the crumbled bayleaves, and the lemon peel. Place the leg of lamb in the dish and baste well with the marinading liquid.

Leave in a cool place for 2–3 days, turning it over and basting as often as you remember, so that it becomes evenly impregnated with the marinade.

When ready to cook, place the meat on a rack in a roasting tin, strain in the marinade, sprinkle the meat with salt and pepper and dot with the butter. Roast in a moderate oven (190C, 375F, Mark 5) allowing 50 minutes to the kilo, 25 minutes to the pound. The meat should be slightly more cooked than is usual for French lamb recipes. Remove to a heated serving or carving dish. Skim excess fat off the roasting dish. Bring the liquid to the boil, adding a little water if necessary, stir well and scrape up any residue in the pan. Strain and serve as gravy.

Note : A shoulder of lamb may be prepared and cooked in the same way, but the butter should be omitted as shoulders usually have quite sufficient fat on them.

Roast Leg of Lamb

GIGOT ROTI

1 leg of lamb (1¼–2½kg, 3–5lb) *salt and freshly ground black*
3–4 cloves garlic *pepper*
280ml (½ pint, 1¼ cups US) *30g (1oz) butter*
water

Peel the garlic and cut each clove into 2 or 3 slivers lengthways. With a sharp, pointed kitchen knife, make shallow incisions into the meat all round the leg and near the bone, and slide a piece of garlic into each one.

Place the leg of lamb on a rack in a roasting tin, pour the water into the tin, sprinkle the meat with salt and pepper and dot with the butter. Roast in the centre of a moderately hot oven (190C, 375F, Mark 5) allowing 40 minutes to the kilo, 20 minutes to the pound. The flesh, when pierced with a skewer, should produce a clear pale liquid, and, when carved, should be pale pink, not grey. Remove to a heated serving or carving dish.

Bring the juices left in the roasting pan to the boil, adding a little more water if necessary, or a little wine, stir well and scrape up any residue from the pan. Strain and serve as gravy.

Note : A shoulder of lamb may be roasted in the same way, but the butter should be omitted as shoulders usually have quite sufficient fat on them.

Casserole of Lamb with Early Summer Vegetables

NAVARIN PRINTANIER

Pink-fleshed young turnips are a characteristic part of this dish, and imported French ones can often be bought in the early summer. However, if they are not available, small courgettes, left whole, can be substituted. Broad beans may also be used instead of peas.

1 shoulder of lamb (1¼–1½kg, 3–3½lb)	*sprig of rosemary*
60g (2oz) butter or dripping	*bayleaf*
2 onions	*½kg (1lb) new potatoes – or more according to appetites*
1 clove garlic	*½kg (1lb) young carrots*
2 tablespoons flour	*½kg (1lb) baby onions*
1 teaspoon sugar	*½kg (1lb) baby turnips*
560ml (1 pint) stock	*½kg (1lb) fresh peas (shelled weight – approx. 1kg (2lb) unshelled)*
salt and freshly ground black pepper	

Cut the meat off the bone and into cubes. (Use the bone and any trimmings to make stock.) Melt the butter or dripping in a flameproof casserole and fry the sliced onions and garlic till golden brown. Remove from the casserole, and quickly sear the meat until it is well coloured on all sides. Remove from the casserole. Sprinkle the flour and sugar into the casserole, stir well and cook over a fairly high heat until the mixture is quite dark brown, but not burned. (The sugar will help to give it colour.) Slowly add the stock, stirring well until you have a smooth sauce. Season generously, return the meat and onions to the casserole, add the herbs, cover and simmer for about 20 minutes, when the meat should be fairly tender.

Prepare the vegetables meanwhile. Very fresh young carrots and potatoes need only be scrubbed, and should not be peeled or scraped.

Add the potatoes and carrots, cover and continue to simmer. After 10 minutes, add the onions and turnips, leave to simmer for a further 15 minutes, then add the peas or beans, and courgettes if these are being used instead of turnips. When these vegetables are cooked, the navarin is ready.

The meat should be tender and all the vegetables just cooked 'à point', and should each have kept their individual flavour and shape. The cooking time given for the vegetables is obviously approximate, as it will vary according to their size, so adjust the time if necessary, and especially if you are using any frozen vegetables.

The sauce should be smooth and reasonably thick, but not too thick. You can add a little stock just before serving if it is on the thick side, or a little beurre manié (see p. 20) if it is too thin.

Braised Sauerkraut with Pork

CHOUCROUTE GARNIE

A speciality of Alsace (hence its affinity to German cooking) and a hearty dish for a cold day. It is not worth making in small quantities, and those given below will feed 10–12 of the hungriest. Some or all the meats and sausages mentioned below may be used, depending on what is available in your local delicatessen or supermarket, but they should all be based on pork and there should be not less than 1kg (2lb) of meat in all.

2kg (4lb) sauerkraut
60g (2oz) pork, goose or duck fat,
 or 110g (4oz) streaky bacon
2 onions
2 carrots
2 cooking apples
2 cloves garlic (optional)
freshly ground black pepper
10 juniper berries

500g (1lb) smoked bacon or
 pork, or salt pork, or loin of
 pork
1 knuckle of ham
1 large garlic sausage
1 spiced pork sausage per person
1 frankfurter per person
250ml ($\frac{1}{2}$ pint, 1$\frac{1}{4}$ cups US)
 white wine or vermouth
280ml ($\frac{1}{2}$ pint, 1$\frac{1}{4}$ cups US) water

Wash the sauerkraut well in several changes of cold water in order to desalt it. Drain and squeeze out the moisture, a handful at a time.

In a large flameproof casserole melt the fat, or render down the streaky bacon, cut into strips. Gently soften the finely chopped onions, carrots, apples and garlic. Put in a layer of half the sauerkraut, sprinkle generously with pepper and a few crushed juniper berries. Lay the smoked bacon or pork and the knuckle of ham on top, cover with the remaining sauerkraut, sprinkle again with pepper and the remaining juniper berries, and pour on the wine and water. The liquid should come just to the top of the sauerkraut. Bring to the boil, cover and either simmer on top of the stove or in a moderate oven (180C, 350F, Mark 4) for about 1 hour. Then add the garlic sausage, and any pork sausages you may be using. Prick the sausages and, if you like, fry pork sausages first. Bury them in the sauerkraut and continue to cook for a further hour. Then add the frankfurters and cook for another half hour.

These cooking times are the minimum — you can go on cooking the dish for about 4 hours altogether, and it will only improve. Add more water if the dish becomes too dry.

Serve on a big platter, with the sauerkraut piled in the centre. Slice the meat and lay the slices over the mound of sauerkraut, and surround the whole with the sausages.

Serve alone, or with plain boiled potatoes, or black rye bread, and some chilled white wine or beer.

Ham in Aspic

JAMBON PERSILLE

A very pretty dish, especially good for a buffet table.

1½–2½kg (3–5lb) piece of bacon (gammon or forehock)	4–5 bayleaves
	2 onions or 6 shallots
2 pig's trotters, calves feet or knuckles of bacon	12 black peppercorns
	1 dessertspoon white wine vinegar
1 bottle white wine	
a good bunch of tarragon and thyme (or 2 good teaspoons dried herbs)	large bunch fresh parsley (60g, 2oz approx.)

Soak the bacon for several hours in cold water. Rinse and put in a large saucepan, cover with cold water, bring slowly to the boil and simmer for 1 hour. Drain and leave to cool a little, then remove the rind.

Blanch the trotters, calves feet or knuckles of bacon, and rinse.

Put the bacon in a clean saucepan, add the trotters, calves feet or knuckles, pour on the wine, add the herbs, onions and peppercorns, and a little water if the wine does not quite cover the ham. Bring slowly to the boil, then keep just above simmering point for 2½–3½ hours, until the ham is very well cooked and ready to fall apart. Skim any fat or scum off the cooking liquid from time to time.

Lift the ham out of the saucepan and strain the cooking liquid into a bowl. Add the vinegar, taste for seasoning and leave to cool.

Mash the ham lightly with a fork and put into a serving bowl – preferably a white one which will show off the pink and green of the final dish.

When the cooking liquid begins to set, skim off any fat from the top, stir in the finely chopped parsley and pour over the ham. Leave overnight in the refrigerator to set.

Once set, you can turn the ham out of the dish on to a plate or slice it in the bowl.

Pork with Apples and Cider

PORC NORMAND

1 kg (2lb) loin of pork or pork
    chops
½kg (1lb) apples
2 onions
salt and freshly ground black
    pepper
2 tablespoons calvados or brandy
    (optional)

140ml (¼ pint, ⅝ cup US) cider
140ml (¼ pint, ⅝ cup US)
    double cream and
140ml (¼ pint, ⅝ cup US) sour
    cream or
280ml (½ pint, 1¼ cups US)
    crème fraîche (see p. 16)

Take the skin and fat off the meat, and remove any bones. Cut
the meat into cubes or strips. Dice the fat finely and render
down.

Peel, core and finely chop the apples. Chop the onions
finely and soften in 2 tablespoons of the pork fat in a deep
frying pan or flameproof casserole. Raise the heat, add the
meat and brown quickly on all sides.

Add the apples and seasoning, lower the heat, cover and
simmer for 20–30 minutes, until the meat is tender and the
apples have cooked down to a thick purée.

Uncover, add the cider and brandy, raise the heat and
allow to bubble fiercely for 1 minute to reduce. Pour in the
cream, stir well and bring back to boil for 1 minute. Check
seasoning before serving.

Note : For a really economical version of this dish, use belly of
pork.

Veal Stewed in Tomatoes and Garlic

AILLADE DE VEAU

1kg (2lb) lean veal (cut from shoulder or shin)
3 tablespoons olive oil
500g (1lb) tomatoes
10 cloves garlic
1 teaspoon dried basil or marjoram

salt and freshly ground black pepper
1 teaspoon sugar
140ml ($\frac{1}{4}$ pint, $\frac{5}{8}$ cup US) white wine
60g (2oz) breadcrumbs
strip of lemon peel
small bunch parsley

Cut the meat into large cubes or strips, and brown in the olive oil in a large flameproof casserole.

Meanwhile peel and roughly chop the tomatoes, and peel and chop the garlic finely. Cook together in a deep frying pan over a moderately high heat until all the liquid has evaporated and the tomatoes are reduced to a thick purée. Add the dried herbs and season generously with the salt, pepper and sugar.

When all the pieces of meat have been browned, pour the wine into the casserole and stir well to loosen the sediment at the bottom of the casserole. Season the meat.

Add the tomato purée to the casserole, cover and simmer over a low flame or cook in a low oven (150C, 300F, Mark 2) for about one hour, or until the meat is tender.

Chop the lemon peel finely together with the parsley, and mix into the breadcrumbs. Put a layer of this mixture over the meat in the casserole and brown quickly in a hot oven or under the grill.

Serve with rice or noodles.

Veal Stew in White Sauce

BLANQUETTE DE VEAU

For this dish it is best to buy the meat in one piece, on the
bone. If ready-cut pie veal has to be used, try to obtain a
knuckle of veal to go with it.

1kg (2lb) shoulder or breast of veal (see above)	225g (½lb) button mushrooms
1 knuckle of veal (see above)	85g (3oz) butter
½ lemon	60g (2oz) flour
1 onion	salt and pepper
1 carrot	2 egg yolks
bouquet garni	140ml (¼ pint, ⅝ cup US)
225g (½lb) button onions	double cream
	parsley

Cut the meat off the bone and cut into cubes (approx. 3cm
(1½in) square). Put into a bowl with the bones, cover with
cold water, add a slice of lemon and leave to soak for 3 or 4
hours, changing the water once or twice. This will blanch the
meat.

Drain the meat, put in a large saucepan together with the
bones, and add enough cold water to cover. Bring slowly to
the boil, then lower the heat and skim off any scum. When the
water begins to clear, add another slice of lemon, the onion,
peeled and roughly chopped, the carrot, scraped and chopped,
and the bouquet garni, and simmer gently for about 1½ hours,
until the meat is very tender.

Meanwhile blanch the peeled button onions for 10 minutes,
until they are just soft but still firm. Wipe and trim the mushrooms and seal in 30g (1oz) of butter for 2 minutes over a high
heat.

When the meat is ready, take it out and keep warm. Strain
the cooking liquid.

In a clean saucepan or flameproof casserole, melt the
remaining butter, add the flour and cook, stirring, for 5
minutes without allowing to brown. Slowly add 1 litre (1¾
pints, 4⅜ cups US) of the cooking liquid, stirring the whole

time, to make a smooth sauce. Add the meat, the onions and mushrooms, season and leave to simmer for 10 minutes.

Beat the cream into the egg yolks, add the juice of the remaining piece of lemon, stir in some of the hot veal sauce, then pour this into the casserole, stirring well. Taste for seasoning and heat through, but do not allow to boil.

Sprinkle with some chopped parsley before serving. Best served with rice.

Note : Use any surplus stock to make Vichyssoise Soup (see p. 44)

Veal Escalopes with Apples

ESCALOPES DE VEAU A LA VALLEE D'AUGE

4 veal escalopes	1 large or 2 medium cooking
salt and freshly ground black	apples
pepper	140ml ($\frac{1}{4}$ pint, $\frac{5}{8}$ cup US) cider
60g (2oz) butter	1 tablespoon calvados or brandy
	1 tablespoon thick cream

Season the escalopes well on both sides and sear quickly in the butter. When they are lightly browned (3 minutes on each side should be enough), remove from the pan and keep warm.

Peel, core and chop the apple quite finely, add to the pan with the cider, stir well to loosen all the sediment and cook over a moderate heat for a few minutes to soften the apple. Add the warmed calvados or brandy and set alight. When the flames have died down, stir in the cream and return the escalopes, and any juice from them, to the pan and heat through before serving.

Note : Veal chops may be cooked in the same way but, after they have been seared on both sides, they will need a little more cooking time, and you will probably wish to increase the amount of apples, cider and cream to make sufficient sauce to cover the rather thicker chops.

Veal Escalopes in Paper Parcels

ESCALOPES DE VEAU EN PAPILLOTES

4 veal escalopes   *225g (8oz) mushrooms*
salt and freshly ground black   *2 small onions or shallots*
*   pepper*   *small bunch parsley*
1 tablespoon olive oil   *small bunch chives*
a good squeeze lemon juice   *30g (1oz) butter*

Season the veal escalopes with salt and pepper, dribble a little olive oil and lemon juice over each one, pile on top of each other and leave to marinade for an hour or two.

Wash and trim the mushrooms and chop finely with the onions or shallots, the parsley and chives. Season the mixture.

Cut a large square of greaseproof paper or foil for each escalope and butter each square well. Lay an escalope on each one, pile on a good helping of the mushroom mixture and fold up the paper or foil to make a neat, well-sealed parcel which will not allow steam or juice to escape.

Lay the parcels side by side on an oven tray and cook in a moderate oven (180C, 350F, Mark 4) for 30 minutes.

Serve in their paper, and allow everyone to unpack his own parcel on the plate.

Calf's Liver with Onions

FOIE DE VEAU A LA LYONNAISE

Lambs' liver cooked in this way is also very delicious and more economical.

500g (1lb) liver   *110g (4oz) butter*
1 tablespoon flour   *salt and pepper*
500g (1lb) onions   *1 tablespoon wine vinegar*

Cut the liver diagonally into thick slices and dust lightly with the flour so that each slice is thinly coated.

Peel and slice the onions into thin rings.

Heat half the butter in a frying pan and when it is foaming and just beginning to turn brown, put in the slices of liver. Turn each slice over as soon as the top surface begins to pearl with blood, and cook on the other side (approximately 2 minutes on each side). Remove to a serving dish, season and keep hot.

Add the remaining butter to the frying pan and when hot, put in the onions and cook over a high flame, stirring frequently, until they are browned. Season the onions, add the vinegar, bring just to the boil and pile over the liver in the serving dish.

Serve hot, with puréed potatoes.

Veal Kidneys in Brandy Sauce

ROGNONS DE VEAU FLAMBES

Though veal kidneys are the most delicate, lambs' or pigs' kidneys may be cooked in the same way.

4 veal or pigs' kidneys, or 6 lambs' kidneys	140ml ($\frac{1}{4}$ pint, $\frac{5}{8}$ cup US) sour cream or
1 medium onion	140ml ($\frac{1}{4}$ pint, $\frac{5}{8}$ cup US) double
110g (4oz) mushrooms	cream and good squeeze of
110g (4oz) butter	lemon juice
1 tablespoon brandy	salt and freshly ground black
2 teaspoons Dijon mustard	pepper

Peel the kidneys, remove the core and cut into very thick slices. Chop the onion finely and slice the mushrooms.

Melt the butter in a frying pan and soften the onion and mushrooms together. Remove from the pan and set aside.

Raise the heat, put kidneys into the frying pan and cook over a moderately high heat, stirring so that they cook evenly, until they have changed colour and are tender (approximately 10 minutes).

Warm the brandy in the spoon, set alight and pour evenly over the kidneys. When the flames have died down, return the onions and mushrooms to the pan, stir in the mustard and then the cream and lemon juice, season to taste and serve very hot.

Serve alone, with a little French bread, or with some plain boiled rice.

Poultry • Les Volailles

The deep yellow, maize-fed chickens of the Bresse district have a flavour that cannot be equalled, but a good free-range chicken will amply repay the trouble lavished on it by the recipes which follow.

I have included a recipe for guinea fowl, because these are becoming more commonly available here, but have not felt it necessary to add recipes for other game birds as the English excel at the cooking of these.

However, I could not resist adding one recipe for hare, since it is utterly delicious and quite unlike any of our usual ways of cooking hare.

Chicken in Red Wine

COQ AU VIN

1 roasting chicken (approx.
1¾kg, 4lb weight)
1 onion
1 carrot
bouquet garni
110g (4oz) lean bacon
85g (3oz) butter
salt and freshly ground black
pepper
30g (1oz) flour
4 tablespoons brandy
560ml (1 pint, 2¼ cups US)
full-bodied red wine
(preferably Burgundy or
Beaujolais)

1 dessertspoon tomato purée
2 cloves garlic
several sprigs of thyme or
½ teaspoon dried thyme
bayleaf
450g (1lb) button onions
225g (8oz) button mushrooms
2 tablespoons olive oil
pinch of sugar
1 teaspoon wine vinegar
6 slices white bread

Joint the chicken and make a stock from the carcass and giblets with the onion, carrot and bouquet garni. Cut the bacon into small strips, melt 15g (½oz) of the butter in a flameproof casserole and fry the bacon in it gently until it begins to give out its fat. Season the pieces of chicken, dust them lightly with some of the flour, add them to the casserole and fry till golden brown on all sides.

Heat the brandy in a small saucepan, pour over the chicken in the casserole, set alight and shake a little so that all the pieces of chicken are covered in flame. When the flames have subsided, pour on the wine and add enough stock to just cover the chicken. Add the tomato purée and the lightly crushed cloves of garlic, the thyme and the bayleaf. Cover and simmer slowly for 20–30 minutes until the chicken is tender, and the juices running from the drumstick when it is pricked with a fork are clear.

Meanwhile, peel and braise the button onions in a heavy saucepan in 30 g (1oz) of the butter and one tablespoon of the olive oil. When they begin to brown, add a pinch of sugar, the vinegar and 2 tablespoons of the chicken stock, cover and simmer until just tender.

Clean the mushrooms. Heat 30g (1oz) of the butter with the second tablespoon of olive oil in a wide, heavy saucepan, and when it begins to bubble, add the mushrooms and cook them over a fairly high heat until they are lightly browned. In this way, they should not give out very much liquid, but should remain crisp and juicy.

When the chicken is ready, lift out of the casserole, place in a deep serving dish and keep hot.

Skim the excess fat off the top of the casserole. Raise the heat and boil the cooking liquid very fast for 5 minutes to reduce. Remove the thyme and bayleaf, and the cloves of garlic if they have not completely disintegrated.

Meanwhile, fry the slices of bread in the fat skimmed off the casserole or in a little butter and another tablespoon of olive oil, until crisp and golden brown. Cut each into 4 triangles.

Make a beurre manié by working the flour into the remaining butter. Stir this slowly into the casserole off the heat, return briefly to the heat and bring just to the boil. Remove once more from the heat. The sauce should now be quite thick and slightly shiny.

Pour the sauce over the chicken in the serving dish (or serve in the casserole). Add the braised onions and mushrooms, and surround with the croutons of fried bread.

Tarragon Chicken

POULET A L'ESTRAGON

This must be made with fresh or frozen tarragon, as the dried herb does not have the same aromatic, slightly bitter, savour. Though fresh tarragon is hard to buy in England, it grows easily in the garden, or in pots or window-boxes, and freezes very well.

1 roasting chicken (approx. 1¾kg, 4lb weight)	140ml (¼ pint, ⅝ cup US) white wine
60g (2oz) butter	4–5 large sprigs of tarragon
1 onion	2 egg yolks
1 carrot	140ml (¼ pint, ⅝ cup US)
1 celery stalk	double cream or crème fraîche
60g (2oz) flour	(see p. 16)
salt and freshly ground black pepper	squeeze of lemon juice

Joint the chicken and make a stock from the carcass and giblets.

Melt the butter in a large flameproof casserole, and gently cook the finely chopped vegetables until they soften. Do not allow them to brown.

Add the chicken pieces and cook them gently, turning from time to time, until they are butter yellow, but not brown. Lift out with a slotted spoon and set aside.

Season the flour liberally with the salt and pepper, then sprinkle into the casserole. Continue to cook over a gentle heat, stirring, for five minutes until the flour is cooked and pale brown.

Remove the casserole from the heat, add the wine and stir well to loosen all the sediment. Return to the heat, bring briefly to the boil, still stirring; return the pieces of chicken to the casserole and add enough chicken stock to just cover.

Add 2 sprigs of the tarragon, cover the casserole and leave to simmer for 20–30 minutes until the chicken is tender and the juices running from the meat, when pricked with a fork, are clear.

Combine the egg yolks with the cream, adding a good squeeze of lemon juice unless you are using crème fraîche.

Lift the pieces of chicken out of the casserole and keep warm. Raise the heat, bring the sauce to the boil, and boil rapidly for 5 minutes to reduce. Begin to beat a little of the sauce into the cream and, when about 140ml ($\frac{1}{4}$ pint, $\frac{5}{8}$ cup US) has been added, pour the cream in a thin stream into the casserole, off the heat, stirring well.

Return the casserole to a moderate heat, and bring slowly to the boil, still stirring. Boil for 1 minute. Add the remaining tarragon leaves, roughly chopped, return the pieces of chicken to the casserole to heat through, and serve.

Chicken in Cheese Sauce

POULET AU GRATIN

1 roasting chicken (approx.
   1$\frac{3}{4}$kg, 4lb weight)
1 knuckle of veal or calf's foot
1 onion
1 carrot
1 clove garlic
bouquet garni
60g (2oz) pork fat or butter
salt and freshly ground black
   pepper

bunch of fresh thyme, marjoram
   and rosemary or 1 teaspoon
   mixed dried herbs
2 tablespoons brandy
140ml ($\frac{1}{4}$ pint, $\frac{5}{8}$ cup US)
   double cream or crème fraîche
   (see p. 16)
1 dessertspoon French mustard
110g (4oz) gruyère cheese

Joint the chicken and make a stock with the carcass and giblets, the knuckle of veal or calf's foot (this is important to give the stock body) and the vegetables and bouquet garni. Simmer for about 1 hour, then strain and reduce liquid to 560ml (1 pint, 2$\frac{1}{2}$ cups US).

Brown the pieces of chicken lightly in the pork fat or butter in a heavy flameproof casserole. Season liberally and add the herbs. Warm the brandy, set it alight and pour over the chicken. When the flames have died down, pour in the stock. Cover and simmer slowly for 30–40 minutes until the chicken is tender, and the juices running from the thickest part of the drumstick, when it is pricked with a fork, are clear. Lift out the pieces of chicken and keep warm. Skim fat off the stock and bring to the boil. Boil briskly for 5 minutes to reduce.

Stir the mustard into the cream, pour on a little of the hot stock and stir well, then take the casserole off the heat and pour in the cream. Stir well, and add half the grated cheese.

Return the chicken to the casserole, sprinkle on the remaining grated cheese and brown quickly in the top of a hot oven or under the grill before serving.

Chicken with Peppers, Tomato and Olives

POULET NICOISE

1 roasting chicken (approx. 1¾kg, 4lb weight)	30g (1oz) butter
1 clove garlic	2 large onions
salt and freshly ground black pepper	500g (1lb) peppers (mixture of red and green)
2 tablespoons olive oil	500g (1lb) tomatoes
	12 black olives

Joint the chicken and rub each piece with the cut surface of the clove of garlic and some salt and pepper.

Heat the oil and butter in a large flameproof casserole and quickly brown the chicken pieces on each side. Remove from the casserole and keep warm.

Lower the heat, add the finely sliced onions and the finely chopped garlic clove to the casserole, stir, cover and cook for 5–10 minutes until soft but not browned. Lay the pieces of chicken on top of the bed of onions, cover and continue to cook over a moderate heat for 10 minutes.

Meanwhile wash the peppers and remove all pith and seeds. Cut into fine strips. Add these to the casserole.

Peel and roughly chop the tomatoes, add these also to the casserole, cover and continue to cook for a further 20–30 minutes until the chicken is tender.

Add the stoned and roughly chopped olives 5 minutes before serving, and taste for seasoning.

Roast Chicken

POULET ROTI

1 roasting chicken (approx.	*1 teaspoon mixed dried herbs*
1¾kg, 4lb weight)	*110g (4oz) butter*
1 clove garlic	*1 onion*
salt and freshly ground black	*1 carrot*
pepper	*strip of lemon peel*

Preheat the oven to 220C (425F, Mark 7).

Wipe the chicken inside and out with a damp cloth or a piece of kitchen paper, and rub all over with the cut surface of the clove of garlic. Rub salt, pepper and herbs round inside, rub plenty of salt into the skin all over the outside of the chicken. Place one quarter of the butter inside the chicken and lay it on its side on a rack in the baking tin. Smear another quarter of the softened butter over the exposed side of the chicken and place it in the centre of the oven. After 15 minutes turn the bird over and smear half the remaining butter over the other side. After another 15 minutes turn the bird on to its back, smear the breast with the remaining butter, and return to the oven again. Turn the oven down to 190C (375F, Mark 5). Cook for another half hour, basting several times.

After one hour's cooking time, the skin should be crisp and golden brown, and the chicken moist, tender and cooked.

Meanwhile, boil the giblets for 20 minutes with the herbs, the roughly cut up onion and carrot and the lemon peel to make approximately 140ml (¼ pint, ⅝ cup US) of stock.

Pour off about half the fat from the roasting tin, then let the juices from inside the bird pour into the tin, remove the bird and set on a heated serving dish or carving board. Leave for at least 5 minutes in a warm place before carving.

Bring the juices in the roasting pan to the boil, slowly strain in the stock from the giblets and boil rapidly to reduce. Thicken with a little beurre manié (see p. 20) if necessary, and test for seasoning before serving the gravy separately.

Duck with Orange

CANETON BIGARADE

To achieve the proper aromatic flavour for this dish, Seville oranges should ideally be used, but as their season is so short, this recipe gives instructions also for making with ordinary oranges. The slight bitterness of the oranges, especially their peel, counteracts the richness and enhances the flavour of the duck, and the dish should have a pleasant hint of tartness, as opposed to the sickly sweetness it too often has when served in English restaurants.

1 large duck	2–3 Seville oranges or 1 sweet
1 clove garlic	Spanish navel orange
salt and pepper	30g (1oz) butter
1 onion	45g (1½oz) flour
1 carrot	140ml (¼ pint, ⅝ cup US) dry
bayleaf	white or red wine
	pinch of sugar

Wipe the duck inside and out, prick the skin all over with a sharp-pronged fork, rub inside and out with the cut surface of the clove of garlic and rub salt liberally into the skin.

Put in a hot oven (220C, 425F, Mark 7) and after 15 minutes turn heat down to 190C (375F, Mark 5), and roast altogether for 1½ hours, or until the juice that runs out when you prick the thickest part of the drumstick is clear or just pale pink. Pour off the fat from time to time.

Meanwhile, make a stock by simmering the duck giblets with plenty of water and the halved onion, the roughly chopped carrot and the bayleaf.

Pare the rind of the oranges very finely (a potato peeler makes this simple) and cut it into very thin strips. Plunge these into boiling water, boil for 3 minutes, then drain.

Quarter of an hour before the duck is ready, begin to make the sauce. Melt the butter in a heavy saucepan, and allow to turn nutty brown. Add the flour, stir well, and cook over a moderate heat until the mixture is pale caramel brown. Add the wine, stir until smooth, then add 420ml (¾ pint, 1⅞ cups

US) of the strained giblet stock. Add the pinch of sugar, season to taste, and stir over a moderate heat until the sauce has thickened.

Carve the duck when ready into serving pieces and arrange these on a heated platter. Add the juices that remain in the roasting tin after skimming off the fat, and the juice that has run from the duck when carving, to the sauce.

Stir in the juice from the oranges and the peel, heat through well and pour over the duck before serving.

Duck with Cherries

CANETON AUX CERISES

1 large duck	*juice ½ lemon*
salt	*3 tablespoons brandy or Marc*
1 onion	*30g (1oz) sugar*
1 carrot	*2 tablespoons red wine vinegar*
bayleaf	*140ml (¼ pint, ⅝ cup US) white*
500g (1lb) cherries, morello if	* wine*
* possible, or 500g (1lb) tin or*	*30g (1oz) butter*
* jar morello cherries*	*45g (1½oz) flour*

Wipe the duck well inside and out, and rub salt liberally into the skin. Prick the skin all over with a sharp-pronged fork.

Place breast side up in a hot oven (220C, 425F, Mark 7) and after 15 minutes turn the oven down to 190C (375F, Mark 5) and roast for a further hour to 1¼ hours or until the juice running out from the thickest part of the drumstick, when pricked with a fork, is clear or palest pink. Pour off the fat from the baking tin from time to time.

Meanwhile, make a stock from the duck giblets with the onion, carrot and bayleaf.

Stone the cherries if necessary, and drain off and set aside the syrup if using tin or jar. Marinade the cherries in the lemon juice and brandy.

Boil the sugar and vinegar together until the liquid evaporates and the mixture turns dark toffee brown. Stir, and watch carefully so that it does not burn. Remove from the heat and at once add 140ml ($\frac{1}{4}$ pint, $\frac{5}{8}$ cup US) of the duck stock. Stir to dissolve the caramel.

When the duck is ready, carve into serving pieces and keep warm in a casserole or on a deep serving platter.

Skim excess fat off the juices in the roasting pan, pour in the white wine and bring to the boil, stirring well to dislodge any sediment. Add the caramelised stock and the marinade from the cherries. Bring rapidly to the boil and reduce a little.

Make a beurre manié (see p. 20) with half the butter and the flour. Add, and stir until the sauce thickens. Cut the remaining butter into small pieces and add to the sauce. Shake until the butter has dissolved. This will give the sauce a rich, glossy look.

Arrange the cherries round the pieces of duck, pour over the sauce and serve.

Roast Guinea Fowl

PINTADE ROTI

The French tend to eat very young guinea fowl, and often serve a whole bird per person. Here the birds are usually rather older and larger, and half a bird per serving is ample.

2 large or 4 small guinea fowl	110g (4oz) streaky bacon
salt and freshly ground black pepper	1 teaspoon red jam
70g (2½oz) butter	140ml (¼ pint, ⅝ cup US) red wine
bunch of fresh herbs	1 tablespoon flour
280ml (½ pint, 1½ cups US) water	

Wipe the guinea fowl inside and out and rub plenty of salt and pepper into the cavities and the skin of the birds. Put a knob of butter inside each bird, together with a small bunch of herbs. Melt all but 15g (½oz) of the remaining butter and rub this all over the birds. Place in a deep roasting tin, add the water and any of the giblets. Cover the breasts with slices of bacon and cook in a moderately hot oven (140C, 375F, Mark 5) for 50–60 minutes, until the birds are cooked.

Remove the birds from the roasting tin and keep warm. Remove the giblets from the roasting tin, bring the stock in it to the boil, add the jam and wine, test for seasoning. Make a beurre manié (see p. 20) from the remaining butter and the flour, and stir into the gravy to thicken. Cook gently for 3 minutes, then serve.

Pigeons with Grapes

PIGEONS A LA VENDANGEUSE

As the name implies, a dish traditionally made at grape harvest time, when the pigeons are also fat and plentiful.

4 pigeons	*750g (1½lb) white or black grapes*
60g (2oz) butter	*2 tablespoons brandy or Marc*
2 onions	*salt and pepper*

Wipe the pigeons inside and out and brown them quickly on all sides in the butter in a flameproof casserole. Remove from the casserole and keep warm. Chop the onions finely and soften in the casserole. Return the pigeons, warm the brandy or marc, pour over the pigeons and set alight. When the flames have died down, add 500g (1lb) of the grapes (there is no need to pip or skin them). Season, cover and cook over a low heat for 1½–2 hours, depending on the age of the birds, until the pigeons are tender.

Take out the pigeons, split in half or carve and keep warm on a deep serving dish.

Pass the sauce through a sieve, bring rapidly to the boil to reduce a little.

Taste for seasoning and pour over the pigeons.

Decorate the dish with the remaining grapes, skinned and pipped, and serve with rice.

Variation : You can use raisins instead of grapes. Use only

225g (½lb) of raisins, and plump them up first by soaking in water overnight. Drain the next day and leave to soak in another tablespoon of brandy or marc for at least ½ hour before cooking.

Roast Saddle of Hare with Cream

RABLE DE LIEVRE A LA CREME

One of the commonest ways of cooking hare in France is in a civet, or stew, very like jugged hare. Here is a more unusual method.

A 'rable' is strictly speaking a saddle, but this can also be made with the saddle and hindlegs, thus being ample for 4 persons.

1 saddle of hare, including the hindlegs	1 teaspoon mixed dried herbs
1 tablespoon olive oil	60g (2oz) butter
salt and freshly ground black pepper	140ml (¼ pint, ⅝ cup US) thick double cream or crème fraîche (see p. 16)
1 teaspoon wine vinegar	

Remove the iridescent inner skin of the hare as far as possible.

Combine olive oil, salt and pepper, vinegar and herbs and drizzle this over the hare in a roasting tin or shallow baking dish. Leave to marinade for several hours, turning occasionally.

When you are ready to cook the hare, melt the butter in a small saucepan, and when sizzling hot pour over the hare. Place in a moderately hot oven (190C, 375F, Mark 5) and cook for 35–40 minutes, basting and turning at quite frequent intervals. On no account must the sediment at the bottom of the roasting tin be allowed to burn, as this will make it turn very bitter.

Remove from the oven, carve the saddle (the meat should be just pink inside) and put on a dish to keep warm.

Add the cream to the roasting tin and bring quickly to the

boil, stirring to scrape up all the sediment. Season and add a
drop more wine vinegar if the sauce seems a little bland.
Pour over the hare and serve.

Eggs • Les Oeufs

The French housewife is at her economical best in this branch of cooking. She excels in creating whole meals with eggs, or light and appetising starters, and will often use no more than three or four to achieve her effects. Here is just a handful from the 685 ways of cooking eggs reputedly known to expert French chefs.

Cheese Puff

GOUGERE

Serve plain, with a salad, as a light lunch or supper dish, or with a hot vegetable piled in the centre, topped with a sauce béchamel, mornay or hollandaise (see pp. 46, 47).

280ml ($\frac{1}{2}$ pint, 1$\frac{1}{4}$ cups US) milk
100g (3$\frac{1}{2}$oz) butter
salt and pepper
125g (4$\frac{1}{2}$oz) flour

4 eggs
110g (4oz) gruyère or sharp
  cheddar cheese

Put the milk into a heavy saucepan with the butter cut into small pieces and the salt and pepper. Bring rapidly to the boil so that the milk and butter amalgamate. Take off the heat and pour in the sifted flour all at once. Stir rapidly until you have a thick paste. Return to a very gentle heat and stir until the mixture leaves the sides of the pan clean.

Take off the heat again and beat in the eggs, one at a time. Do not add the next egg until the previous one has become completely absorbed.

Cut the cheese into small cubes, and stir in all but one tablespoon of the cubes.

Butter a baking sheet and spoon on half the mixture in a wide circle. Pile the rest on in a circle round the edge to form a kind of nest shape. Or use a buttered ring mould. Scatter on the remaining cheese.

Bake in the centre of a moderately hot oven (190C, 375F, Mark 5) for 35–40 minutes, until the top has risen and is golden brown, and the gougère is firm to the touch. Serve immediately.

Eggs with Ham and Sauce

OEUFS BENEDICTINES

There are several interpretations of this classic dish, which can be served as a starter or light lunch or supper dish. The most usual is the version given here, but the ham may be omitted or replaced by a spoonful of brandade de morue (see p. 56) and, if you wish to be very correct, the base should be a round of cooked pâte brisée (see p. 18) or puff pastry.

4 eggs
4 rounds white bread
butter

4 slices of ham
6 tablespoons sauce hollandaise
(see p. 47)

Poach or coddle the eggs and keep warm. Toast the slices of bread lightly on one side. Butter the untoasted side generously, place a slice of ham and then one egg on each, cover with the hollandaise and serve.

Baked Eggs

OEUFS EN COCOTTE

1 egg per person
butter

1 tablespoon double cream per egg
salt and freshly ground pepper

Put a knob of butter into each individual ramekin or cocotte dish, place in a moderate oven (190C, 375F, Mark 5) for a few minutes to heat through and allow the butter to melt. Carefully break one egg into each dish, pour a tablespoon of cream over each egg and return to the oven for 15 minutes. This should be just enough to set the whites of the egg to a creamy consistency, leaving the yolks still runny. As oven temperatures vary a little, watch carefully so that the eggs are not over-cooked, which will make them leathery, nor under-cooked, which is equally unpalatable.

Season lightly before bringing to the table.

Note : To make this a more substantial dish, place a small slice of pâté in the bottom of each dish before breaking in the egg.

Coddled Eggs with Herbs

OEUFS MOLLETS AUX FINES HERBES

1–2 eggs per person   *fresh herbs – parsley, chives,*
15g (½oz) butter per egg   *tarragon*
lemon juice

Boil the eggs for just 4 minutes, remove immediately from the heat and run cold water over them. As soon as they are cool enough to handle, crack the shell all over very gently. Leave in cold water till quite cold, then shell very carefully.

Just before serving, melt the butter so that it becomes hot but does not burn. Put in the eggs, roll them about in the saucepan so that they heat through evenly and quite fast. Add a good squeeze of lemon juice and about 1 teaspoon of the freshly chopped herbs per egg. Serve immediately.

Foamy Omelette

OMELETTE SOUFFLE

This is also called Omelette Poulard, being a speciality of the famous restaurant La Mère Poulard, which nestles at the foot of the Mont St Michel. Here it is served in mid-meal, between the fish and the meat course, but most of us would find it ample as a first course, or as a simple lunch or supper dish. It can, of course, be stuffed with bits of chicken or fish (a very little lobster would put the dish into the luxury class), but it is also quite delicious served plain.

The quantity given here makes two omelettes, using a 22–25cm (9–10in) omelette pan. It is best not to make too many omelettes at a time, as they should be eaten very fresh.

4 eggs   *salt and freshly ground black*
30g (1oz) butter   *pepper*

Separate the eggs. Beat the yolks with plenty of seasoning, and whip the whites till they stand in peaks, but are not quite dry. Fold into the yolks.

Heat the omelette pan over a high heat, lower the heat a little and add half the butter. Swirl round the pan and, when it is sizzling, but has not changed colour, pour in half the omelette mixture. Shake the pan a little and, as the omelette begins to set, scrape the bottom of the pan gently here and there with a fork, run a palette knife round the edges, and lift it slightly. As soon as the bottom of the omelette has reached the required golden brown colour, lift with the palette knife and carefully fold one half over the other.

Slide onto a heated plate, and make the second omelette in the same way. The omelettes should be golden brown and slightly crisp on the outside, and lightly set in the middle, with the creamy centre gently oozing out at the edges.

Ragoût of Peppers and Tomatoes with Eggs

PIPERADE

500g (1lb) onions
500g (1lb) tomatoes
500g (1lb) peppers (a mixture of red, gold and green if possible)
2 cloves garlic (optional)
110g (4oz) butter
1 tablespoon olive oil
1 teaspoon finely chopped parsley or basil
6 eggs
salt and freshly ground pepper

Peel and slice the onions. Skin the tomatoes and chop them roughly. Halve and wash the peppers, removing all the pith and seeds. Cut them into quite thick strips. Chop the garlic.

In a deep frying pan or flameproof casserole, melt the butter and oil, and cook the onions and garlic over a moderate heat until they are golden but not browned. Add the peppers and continue to cook until they are just soft. Add the tomatoes and herbs and cook until most of the moisture has evaporated. Season to taste.

Beat the eggs together with a little more salt and pepper, and pour into the pan. Stir gently as you would for making scrambled eggs, and when the mixture begins to set, but while it is still creamy, remove from the heat, taste for seasoning, sprinkle with a little more finely chopped herbs and serve.

Triangles of fried bread served with this make it a more substantial dish.

Note : You can also make a kind of pipérade using left-over ratatouille (see p. 125).

Bacon and Egg Tart

QUICHE LORRAINE

200g (7oz) pâte brisée (half the quantity given on p. 18)	*1 small onion*
	3 eggs
60g (2oz) smoked bacon	*280ml (½ pint, 1¼ cups US)*
15g (½oz) butter	*single cream*
60g (2oz) cheese, preferably gruyère or a strong cheddar	*salt and freshly ground black pepper*

Line a buttered 20–22cm (8–9in) flan tin with the pastry, prick and bake blind in a moderately hot oven (190C, 375F, Mark 5) for 10 minutes.

Meanwhile cut the bacon into thin strips and cook gently for 3 minutes in the butter. Drain and spread evenly over the pastry case.

Chop the onion finely, and soften in the butter and bacon fat. Spread this over the bacon.

Grate the cheese or cut into very fine slices and layer this over the bacon and onion.

Break the eggs into a bowl and whisk lightly with a fork to amalgamate. Beat in the cream and season well. Pour into the pastry case.

(You can freeze the quiche at this stage if you wish to. Cook straight from the freezer, allowing 20–30 minutes longer cooking time.)

Return to a shelf above the centre of the oven and bake at the same temperature as above for 35–40 minutes, by which time the eggs should be creamily set and a golden crust have formed on top.

Serve immediately or keep hot for up to 10 minutes in the turned off oven, with the door left open. The quiche may also be served cold.

Instead of making one large quiche, you can also make small individual ones. These will need only 20–25 minutes cooking time.

Variation : Though Quiche Lorraine is the most classic of these open tarts, the bacon can be replaced with chicken or flaked fish, and vegetarian tarts, using cooked spinach or asparagus, or lightly fried slices of courgettes, are also excellent.

Cheese Soufflé

SOUFFLE AU FROMAGE

This makes a simple and economical supper dish, or, baked in individual ramekin dishes, an excellent light starter for a more elaborate meal. Really very easy to make, in spite of its reputation.

110g (4oz) butter	*4 eggs*
60g (2oz) flour	*110g (4oz) grated cheese –*
560ml (1 pint, 2½ cups US) milk	*gruyère or cheddar*
salt and white pepper	*½ tablespoon fine breadcrumbs*

Melt the butter in a large saucepan, add the flour and stir until smooth. Continue to stir over a low heat for 5 minutes, then slowly add the milk, stirring well, until you have a smooth thick sauce; remove from the heat and season.

Separate the eggs and stir the yolks into the sauce one by one, then stir in the grated cheese. You can prepare the soufflé up to this stage well ahead of time.

Beat the egg whites until quite stiff and fold into the sauce, which should be warm but not hot, so reheat first very gently if necessary.

Preheat the oven to 190C (375F, Mark 5). Butter a 1 litre

(2 pint) soufflé or ovenproof dish, and sprinkle the inside
with the breadcrumbs, or prepare individual ramekin dishes.
Pour in the soufflé mixture, and bake in the preheated oven
for 20 minutes for individual soufflés or 35–40 minutes for one
large one. The soufflé should have risen to about twice its
original height, be brown and lightly crusted on top, creamy
in the centre. Serve immediately.

Vegetables • Les Légumes

A French vegetable market is a joy to visit at almost any time of the year, with its loving display of a huge variety of products, each item looking as though it has been individually arranged and polished.

The French cook will take as much trouble with the vegetables as with the meat, and 'les légumes' are often served on their own, after the meat course, so that their individual flavour can be fully appreciated.

Baked Aubergines

AUBERGINES AU GRATIN

The quantities given here are sufficient to make this a first course for 3–4 persons, or a vegetable side dish for up to 6.

1kg (2lb) aubergines	*½ teaspoon sugar*
500g (1lb) tomatoes	*salt and freshly ground black*
60g (2oz) parsley	*pepper*
1 clove garlic	*60g (2oz) breadcrumbs*
125g (4½oz) butter	

Wash and dice the aubergines without peeling. Sprinkle with salt and leave in a colander to drain for 1 hour. Rinse and dry.

Skin and roughly chop the tomatoes. Chop the parsley finely with the garlic.

Melt 15g (½oz) butter in a frying pan and cook the tomatoes over a moderate heat with the parsley and garlic mixture and the sugar, until they have lost all their moisture and have cooked to a thick purée. Season well and set aside.

When the aubergines are ready, fry them gently in 85g (3oz) of the butter until they are soft and have changed colour, but not browned. Transfer to an ovenproof dish, spread on the tomato purée, cover with the breadcrumbs, dot with the remaining butter and cook in the top of a hot oven (220C, 425F, Mark 7) for 20 minutes until the top is golden brown.

Note : Courgettes may also be cooked in the same manner, and are equally delicious.

Baked Beetroot

LES BETTERAVES AU FOUR

This way of cooking beetroot really preserves their flavour.

500g (1lb) beetroot	salt and freshly ground black
15g (½oz) butter	pepper
squeeze of lemon juice	

Wash the beetroot and cut off the leaves, leaving about 2cm (1in) of stalks. Do not peel. Put in an ovenproof casserole, dot with butter, cover and bake in a moderate oven (190C, 375F, Mark 5) for 45 minutes–1½ hours, depending on the size, until they are tender.

When the beetroot are cooked, peel and quarter or slice them, return to the casserole, add the squeeze of lemon juice, a little salt and plenty of pepper, and serve.

The beetroot may also be served with a sauce béchamel (see p. 46).

Carrots

CAROTTES VICHY

Carrots were apparently originally cooked in this way using Vichy water, but tap water will do just as well.

450g (1lb) carrots	salt and freshly ground black
1 tablespoon water	pepper
30g (1oz) butter	1 tablespoon finely chopped
½ teaspoon sugar	parsley

Peel or scrape the carrots. Leave young carrots whole, cut older ones into thick rings. Put into a heavy saucepan with all the other ingredients except the parsley, cover and cook over a gentle heat until just tender, stirring from time to time. This will take anything between 10 and 35 minutes, depending on the size and age of the carrots.

Sprinkle with the parsley just before serving.

Courgettes with Herbs

COURGETTES AUX FINES HERBES

Fresh herbs are essential for this dish, which brings out the delicate flavour of the courgettes.

500g (1lb) courgettes
60g (2oz) butter
lemon juice
salt and freshly ground pepper

1 teaspoon finely chopped fresh
herbs – parsley, chervil,
tarragon or basil

Wash the courgettes but do not peel them. Slice thickly or, if the courgettes are a little on the large side, dice them. Sprinkle with salt and leave in a colander to drain for 1 hour. Rinse and dry.

Melt half the butter in a heavy saucepan or small frying pan, add the courgettes, cover and cook over a gentle heat until they are soft. Stir from time to time. When cooked, the courgettes should be very tender, and a translucent gold but not browned. This will take 20–30 minutes.

Make a herb butter by working the chopped herbs into the remaining butter.

Remove the courgettes from the heat, add a good squeeze of lemon juice, season to taste and dot with the herb butter. Shake the pan well so that the herb butter will melt just sufficiently to form a thick, creamy sauce. Serve at once in a preheated dish.

Chicory (or Belgian Endives)

LES ENDIVES

700g (1½lb) endives (allow 1–2   1 tablespoon lemon juice
   per person)   salt and freshly ground black
60g (2oz) butter   pepper

Wash the endives under plenty of running cold water, discard any discoloured outer leaves and trim off the base. Place them side by side in a thickly buttered shallow ovenproof dish just large enough to hold them, sprinkle with the lemon juice and plenty of salt and pepper, dot with the remaining butter, cover with a lid or double thickness of foil and cook in a moderate oven (180C, 350F, Mark 4) for about one hour, or until the endives are tender.

Alternatively, the endives may be braised in a heavy saucepan, in which case they will not take more than 20–30 minutes, but must be watched to see they do not burn. It may be necessary to add a little water.

Variation

Chicory in a Cheese Sauce

ENDIVES MORNAY

Cover the braised endives with a sauce mornay (see p. 46), sprinkle with a little cheese, dot with a little butter and brown quickly in the top of a hot oven or under a hot grill.

Note : Leeks may also be cooked and served in the same ways.

Spinach Purée

LES EPINARDS EN PUREE

This is not only excellent served as a separate vegetable, it may also be used as a bed for poached eggs or a filling for a quiche; a spoonful can be folded into an omelette or several spoonfuls added to the basic sauce of a cheese soufflé.

1¼kg (2½lb) fresh spinach	*salt and freshly ground black*
cooking salt	*pepper*
110g (4oz) butter	*pinch of nutmeg*

Wash the spinach in several changes of cold water, and pick off any yellow or wilted leaves. Tear off the coarser stalks of large leaves. Fill your largest saucepan with salted water and bring to the boil. Put in all the spinach, a handful at a time, and boil rapidly, uncovered, for 5 minutes. Drain at once through a colander, rinse with cold water, then press out as much water as you can with your hands.

Chop the spinach finely, or put through a mouli or, if you like a very fine purée, through a blender.

Melt the butter in a clean pan, add the spinach and cook over quite a high heat for several minutes, stirring well, until all the water has evaporated and all the butter has been absorbed. Season to taste and add the nutmeg.

Variations

Spinach Purée with Cream

LES EPINARDS A LA CREME

Cook the spinach as for the previous recipe but stir in 2 tablespoons of double cream or crème fraîche (see p. 16) at the end. Heat through before serving.

Sorrel

L'OSEILLE

Sorrel may be cooked in the same way as spinach, and it has a refreshingly astringent flavour.

Turnips with Sugar

NAVETS AU SUCRE

500g (1lb) turnips   30g (1oz) sugar
30g (1oz) butter   salt and freshly ground black
70ml (⅛ pint, ¼ cup US) water   pepper
   or stock   parsley

Wash and peel the turnips. Leave small turnips whole, slice
or dice large ones.

Melt the butter and sugar together over a low heat, add the
turnips and fry gently, without allowing to brown, for 5
minutes. Add the water or stock, season well, cover and cook
until the turnips are tender (10–20 minutes, depending on
size).

Sprinkle with the finely chopped parsley before serving.

*Note : Kohlrabi may be cooked in the same way, but must be
peeled.*

Peas

PETITS POIS A LA FRANCAISE

This method of cooking will give even frozen peas a wonderful
flavour, but it is best when made with fresh-picked garden
peas.

750g (1½lb) peas, shelled weight   60g (2oz) butter
   (approx. 1½kg, 3lb whole peas)   1 teaspoon sugar
2 hearts of lettuce or 1 medium   salt and freshly ground black
   sized lettuce   pepper
3–4 large spring onions, or 1   140ml (¼ pint, ⅝ cup US) water
   small onion   or chicken stock

Pod the peas, wash and shred the lettuce coarsely, peel and
cut the onions into fine rings.

Melt the butter in a saucepan, and soften the onion. Add

the sugar, salt and pepper, put in half the shredded lettuce, add the peas, cover with the remaining lettuce, add the liquid, cover tightly with the lid of the pan, bring to the boil, then simmer for 20–30 minutes, or until the peas are tender.

Serve with any of the cooking liquid which has not evaporated: it is especially delicious.

Braised Potatoes

POMMES DE TERRE CHATEAU

This method is particularly suitable for small, new potatoes, but old ones may be used, provided they are fairly small and of roughly even size. They must also be a smooth round or oval (cut them to shape if necessary) so that they can roll in the pan.

1kg (2lb) potatoes (see above)   *60g (2oz) duck or goose fat*
60g (2oz) butter and   *salt and pepper*
1 tablespoon oil or

Peel the potatoes (very fresh new ones may be left unpeeled) and dry them well on a cloth.

Melt the butter and oil or the fat in a heavy flameproof casserole or saucepan large enough to allow all the potatoes to lie on the bottom. Add the potatoes, roll them a little so that they become evenly covered with the fat, cover closely and cook over a low heat for about 1–1½ hours, depending on the variety and size of the potatoes. Roll them around from time to time, and make sure they are not catching on the bottom of the pan.

When cooked, the potatoes should have a crisp golden brown crust and be meltingly tender inside.

Scalloped Potatoes

POMMES DE TERRE GRATINEES DAUPHINOISES

Use a floury, King Edward-type of potato for this dish.

1kg (2lb) potatoes
½ clove garlic
salt and freshly ground black
*   pepper*

60g (2oz) butter
110g (4oz) grated cheese
*   (gruyère or mild cheddar)*
280ml (½ pint, 1¼ cups US) milk

Peel the potatoes and slice them across into slices approximately ¼cm (⅛in) thick. Leave in cold water for at least 10 minutes to extract the starch, rinse well and pat them dry on a clean teatowel.

Rub the inside of a shallow ovenproof dish with the cut surface of the clove of garlic, and butter the dish lightly. Place a layer of the potato slices in the bottom of the dish, sprinkle with salt and pepper, dot with a little butter and sprinkle with a little grated cheese. Repeat until all the potatoes have been used up. Dot the top layer with the remaining butter and cheese. Bring the milk to the boil, pour on, and cook on the top shelf of a moderately hot oven (200C, 400F, Mark 6) for 1–1½ hours.

The potatoes should be meltingly creamy, with all the butter and milk absorbed, and the top layer lightly browned.

These potatoes are particularly good with poultry or veal.

Variations

Savoyard Potatoes

POMMES DE TERRE GRATINEES SAVOYARD

Substitute stock for milk, add 2–3 finely sliced onions and add a little more butter than for the previous recipe.

Savoyard potatoes are especially good with beef or game.

Potatoes Anna

POMMES DE TERRE GRATINEES ANNA

Substitute cream for the milk, but do not allow the cream to come to the boil. Bring it to just below simmering point before pouring over the potatoes, and cook at a slightly lower heat (190C, 375F, Mark 5). Allow about 2 hours' cooking time.

This is the richest and most mouthwatering version of the dish, delicious with chicken, turkey or pheasant.

Mixed Vegetable Ragoût

RATATOUILLE

Serve hot as a vegetable dish, or cold as an hors d'oeuvre.

2 large aubergines (500g, 1lb approx.)

3–4 courgettes (225g, ½lb approx.)

2 large peppers, 1 red, 1 green if possible (357g, just over ¾lb)

2 large onions (375g, just over ¾lb approx.)

2 cloves garlic (optional)

4 tomatoes (375g, just over ¾lb approx.)

70ml (⅛ pint, ¼ cup US) olive oil

salt and freshly ground black pepper

parsley

Wash the aubergines, cut off the tops and tails but do not peel. Cut into slices ½cm (¼in) thick, sprinkle with salt and leave to drain in a colander for 1 hour. Do the same with the courgettes.

Halve the peppers, wash out all the seeds with great care, and cut into ½cm (¼in) thick strips. Peel and slice the onions and garlic, skin the tomatoes and chop them roughly.

When the aubergines and courgettes are ready, rinse them and squeeze out any excess moisture. Pat dry on kitchen paper.

Heat the oil in a flameproof casserole over a gentle heat and cook the onions and garlic until they are soft. Add the aubergines and cook, stirring well, until they become soft and yellow. Then add the courgettes and peppers, cover and cook gently for ½ hour. Add the tomatoes and seasoning, and cook for another ½ hour without the lid. The vegetables should all be soft, but not have lost their separate identities, and most of the liquid should be evaporated.

Any left-over ratatouille may be used to make pipérade (see p. 112).

Stuffed Baked Tomatoes

TOMATES A LA PROVENCALE

1kg (2lb) large, ripe tomatoes	*2–3 cloves garlic*
salt and freshly ground black	*a large bunch parsley*
pepper	*2 tablespoons dried breadcrumbs*
2 onions	*2 tablespoons olive oil*

Cut the tomatoes in half crosswise. Using a sharp knife, score a criss-cross of lines across each cut surface, and sprinkle liberally with salt and pepper.

Chop the onions, garlic and parsley together until you have a fine hash, then mix into the breadcrumbs. Spread this mixture over the tomatoes and press in well. Place side by side in a shallow oven-proof earthenware dish, or in a baking tin, and cook under a hot grill or in the top of a very hot oven for 15–20 minutes, until the tomatoes are soft and a little charred around the edges.

Jerusalem Artichokes

LES TOPINAMBOURS

Jerusalem artichokes can be cooked in many of the ways in which potatoes are cooked – boiled, mashed or roasted, but they are especially good braised, as below.

1kg (2lb) Jerusalem artichokes	*squeeze of lemon juice*
60g (2oz) butter	*salt and pepper*

Wash and peel the artichokes and cut into roughly even-sized pieces.

Melt the butter in a heavy saucepan or a flameproof casserole, add the artichokes, the lemon juice and salt and pepper, cover and cook over a moderate heat for 30–40 minutes, until the artichokes are tender. Shake the pan from time to time, and if necessary add a little water to stop them from catching.

Check seasoning before serving.

Variations

Jerusalem Artichokes with Cream

TOPINAMBOURS A LA CREME

Stir in 3 tablespoons of double cream or crème fraîche (see p. 16) when the artichokes are cooked. Heat through and sprinkle with a little finely chopped parsley before serving.

Jerusalem Artichokes Stewed in Olive Oil

TOPINAMBOURS A LA PROVENCALE

Use olive oil instead of butter, add one onion and one clove of garlic, finely chopped, and after half an hour add 250g (½lb) tomatoes, peeled and chopped.

Desserts • Les Desserts

The French do not have our tradition of filling 'puddings', and most meals end with cheese and fruit, and perhaps yogurt for the children. But the big Sunday family lunch will often conclude with a large fruit tart – home-made, or bought on the way home from church at the local patissier.

Other desserts – in the home, though not of course in restaurants – are for special occasions, and therefore tend to be elaborate and often very rich concoctions.

Rum Babas

BABA AU RHUM

For the baba
225g (8oz) flour
pinch of salt
15g (½oz) yeast
30g (1oz) caster sugar
140ml (¼ pint, ⅝ cup US) milk
4 eggs
110g (4oz) butter

For the rum syrup
170g (6oz) sugar

420ml (¾ pint, 1⅞ cups US)
   water
2 strips thinly pared lemon or
   orange rind
4 tablespoons rum

To finish
140ml (¼ pint, ⅝ cup US)
   whipped cream or crème
   chantilly (see p. 17)
glacé cherries (optional)

Sift the flour and salt into a large, warm mixing bowl and make a well in the centre.

Cream the yeast with one teaspoon of the sugar, then stir in the warmed milk. Pour into the centre of the bowl, and with a wooden spoon begin to work it into the flour. Beat or knead well for 5–10 minutes, until the mixture ceases to be sticky and leaves the sides of the bowl clean.

Cover the bowl with a damp cloth and leave to rise in a warm, draught-free spot until it has risen to twice its original volume.

Butter some baba tins if you have them. These are either small cylindrical moulds, 5cm (2in) wide and 5cm (2in) deep, or small ring-shaped moulds. If you don't have these, deep patty or fairy cake tins will do quite well.

Melt the butter and let it cool. Whisk the eggs lightly with the remaining sugar and whisk in the butter. Beat this slowly into the dough and continue beating until the mixture becomes smooth and glossy. Half fill each mould with the mixture, and leave to rise again in a warm, draught-free spot until the dough has risen to the top of the moulds.

Bake in a hot oven (220C, 425F, Mark 7) for 15–20 minutes. The babas should be lightly browned on top, quite firm to the touch, and have shrunk away a little from the sides of the moulds. Leave to cool for a few minutes, then turn out upside down on to a cake rack to cool. The babas are ready for their 'baptism' when they are still just warm to the touch.

(The babas may be stored in a tin for a few days, or in the freezer for longer periods, at this point. If so, however, they must be warmed through in a gentle oven before the next procedure takes place.)

Make the syrup by boiling the sugar and water with the lemon or orange strip for 5 minutes. Leave to cool, remove the strips of peel and, when lukewarm, add 3 tablespoons of the rum.

Place the slightly warm babas on a large dish, and pour the lukewarm syrup over them, a little at a time, so that they soak up the maximum of syrup. They should be very moist and spongy, but keep their shape. When they seem to have absorbed as much syrup as they can, lift them carefully on to a cake rack placed over a dish, and leave to drain for ¼ hour. Pour the drained syrup back over the babas.

Sprinkle each baba with a few more drops of rum just before serving, top them or fill the centre of each ring with a spoonful of whipped cream or crème chantilly, and place a glacé cherry in the middle.

Savarin

A savarin is made in the same way as the preceding babas, but it is cooked in one large savarin or ring mould.

For the baba
225g (8oz) flour
pinch of salt
15g (½oz) yeast
30g (1oz) caster sugar
140ml (¼ pint, ⅝ cup US) milk
4 eggs
110g (4oz) butter
60g (2oz) mixed dried fruit or peel (optional)

For the syrup
170g (6oz) sugar

420ml (¾ pint, 1⅞ cups US) water
2 strips thinly pared lemon rind
4 tablespoons Kirsch

To finish
12 glacé cherries
12 blanched almonds
4 tablespoons apricot jam
280ml (½ pint, 1¼ cups US) whipped cream or crème chantilly (see p. 17)

Make the savarin mixture in the same way as for the babas, and fold in the mixed fruit and peel just before pouring the mixture into the mould.

Use a savarin or ring mould 23–25cm (9–10in) diameter. Bake in a moderate oven (190C, 375F, Mark 5) for 35–40 minutes.

When ready, baptise the savarin with a syrup to which Kirsch has been added instead of rum, and decorate with the glacé cherries and blanched almonds.

Melt the apricot jam over a gentle heat, press through a sieve and paint over the savarin to give it a glaze.

Fill the centre of the ring with the lightly whipped cream or crème chantilly, flavoured with a little more Kirsch if you like, just before serving.

Variation

Savarin Montmorency

Fill the centre with a compote of cherries (tinned or bottled will do very nicely) and soak the savarin with their syrup, lightly warmed and flavoured with kirsch. Top with the whipped cream.

Coffee Praliné Cream

BAVAROIS PRALINE

60g (2oz) sugar
60g (2oz) blanched almonds
4 eggs
140g (5oz) caster sugar
½ teaspoon cornflour
420ml (¾ pint, 1⅞ cups US) milk
6 teaspoons instant coffee powder

3 tablespoons boiling water
15g (½oz) powdered gelatine
2 tablespoons brandy, rum or
    liqueur (optional)
140ml (¼ pint, ⅝ cup US)
    double cream

Begin by making the praliné. Melt the sugar in a small, heavy saucepan, and as soon as it turns liquid, add the almonds. Stir well to coat all the almonds and continue to cook until the sugar turns golden brown. Remove from the heat and pour the mixture immediately on to a lightly oiled wooden board. It will harden as it cools. When quite cold, peel off the board and crush to a fine powder with a rolling pin.

Separate the eggs and beat the yolks with half the caster sugar and the cornflour until thick and fluffy. Scald the milk and pour slowly on to the egg mixture, while continuing to beat. Return the custard to the saucepan and cook over a very gentle heat, stirring continuously, until the custard begins to thicken and just coats the back of the spoon. Do not allow to boil. Remove from the heat.

Dissolve the coffee in the boiling water and sprinkle on the gelatine. Leave to soften for a few minutes, then stir into the custard which should still be hot enough to dissolve the gelatine; stir well and leave to cool.

When the custard is cool but has not yet set, stir in half the praliné powder and the brandy, rum or liqueur. Whisk the egg whites until they stand in peaks, then whisk in the remaining caster sugar. Fold into the custard. Whip the cream lightly and fold this in also.

Pour into a glass or soufflé dish and leave to set in the refrigerator.

Sprinkle on the remaining praliné powder before serving.

Coffee Ice-cream with Cream

CAFE LIEGOIS

A really rich dessert or tea-time treat.

280ml ($\frac{1}{2}$ pint, 1$\frac{1}{4}$ cups US)
water
110g (4oz) sugar
4 teaspoons instant coffee

140ml ($\frac{1}{4}$ pint, $\frac{5}{8}$ cup US) crème
fraîche (see p. 16) or double
or whipping cream
280ml ($\frac{1}{2}$ pint, 1$\frac{1}{4}$ cups US)
coffee ice-cream

Boil the sugar and water together for 5 minutes to make a fairly thick syrup. Remove from the heat and stir in the instant coffee. Leave to cool, then chill in the refrigerator.

Whip the crème fraîche with sufficient water to make a very light whipped cream. Do not sweeten, as the slight acidulity makes a specially pleasant contrast to the sweetness and richness of the other ingredients. For this reason also, crème fraîche is infinitely preferable here to ordinary double or whipping cream.

Chill a wine or sundae glass for each person.

When you are ready to serve, spoon a helping of ice-cream into each glass, pour over a little of the coffee syrup and top with a good dollop of the cream. For a really professional look, pipe the cream on through the nozzle of a forcing bag.

Serve, if you like, with some tuiles (see p. 156) or wafers.

Pears Poached in Red Wine

COMPOTE DE POIRES AU VIN ROUGE

A very good way to use cooking or under-ripe pears.

$\frac{1}{2}$kg (1lb) small pears
squeeze of lemon juice
140ml ($\frac{1}{4}$ pint, $\frac{5}{8}$ cup US) water
110g (4oz) sugar

strip of lemon peel
stick of cinnamon
140ml ($\frac{1}{4}$ pint, $\frac{5}{8}$ cup US) (or
more) red wine

Peel the pears but leave them whole, and leave on the stalks.

Keep in a bowl of cold water to which you have added the squeeze of lemon juice until you are ready to use them.

Bring the water and sugar to the boil with the lemon peel and stick of cinnamon in a saucepan that is just large enough to allow all the pears to lie on the bottom. Boil briskly for 3 minutes. Add the pears to the saucepan, pour on enough red wine to cover and poach gently until the pears are soft, but have not lost their shape. This will take anything from 15 minutes to an hour, depending on how hard the pears are.

Lift the pears out with a slotted spoon and place in a serving bowl. Bring the cooking liquid to the boil and boil briskly for 10 minutes, until it has considerably reduced and has the consistency of a light syrup.

Strain this over the pears and leave them to cool in the syrup, turning them from time to time so that they colour evenly.

Serve chilled. A little lightly whipped cream, which may be flavoured with kirsch, served separately, is particularly good with this dish.

Caramel Cream

CREME RENVERSEE AU CARAMEL

170g (6oz) sugar
4 eggs or 3 whole eggs and
2 yolks

½ litre (scant 1 pint, 2¼ cups US)
milk

Melt 110g (4oz) of the sugar in a small heavy saucepan and as as soon as it turns a rich golden brown pour into a 1 litre (2 pint) ovenproof dish. Turn the dish so that bottom and sides are coated with caramel and leave to set.

Beat the eggs and the remaining sugar lightly with a fork. Scald the milk and pour on to the eggs, stirring well to amalgamate and to melt the sugar. Strain this mixture into the caramel-coated dish.

Set the dish in a bain-marie (see p. 19) and cook in a moderate oven (180C, 350F, Mark 4) for about one hour, or until a knife inserted into the cream comes out clean. Leave to cool and then chill in the refrigerator.

Turn out into a deep dish, taking care not to spill the syrup, and serve with a little single cream handed separately.

Crêpes Suzette

A restaurant spectacular which is very easy to make at home.

For the crêpes	For the sauce
140g (5oz) flour	3 oranges
1 tablespoon icing sugar	4 lumps sugar
2 eggs	1 lemon
140ml (¼ pint, ⅝ cup US) milk	60g (2oz) sugar
140ml (¼ pint, ⅝ cup US) water	110g (4oz) butter
60g (2oz) butter	2 tablespoons Grand Marnier or
1 tablespoon brandy	Orange curaçao
	1 tablespoon caster sugar
	2 tablespoons brandy

Make the pancakes by sifting the flour and icing sugar into a bowl, make a well in the centre and add the lightly beaten eggs. Begin to work the flour into the eggs, and add first milk, then water. Beat well until you have a smooth batter. Add the melted butter and the brandy, beat in and leave to rest in the refrigerator for at least 2 hours.

If you have an electric blender you can make the batter very simply by putting all the ingredients in together, starting with the milk and water, then the eggs and then the remaining ingredients. Blend at high speed till smooth and leave to rest.

When you are ready to make the crêpes, give the batter another good beat. Make the pancakes as thinly as possible, by tilting the pan all round when you first pour in the batter. If you have a well-proved pancake pan, you need do no more than grease it very lightly, as the batter contains butter. This quantity makes about twelve 20cm (8in) pancakes.

Make the sauce by rubbing the sugar lumps over 2 of the oranges until they are completely impregnated with the oil of the skins. Peel the rind very thinly off the third orange and cut into very fine strips.

Put the juice and rind of the oranges, the juice of the lemon, the sugar lumps, the sugar, butter and Grand Marnier or orange curaçao in a deep frying pan or chafing dish and bring to the boil, stirring well. Allow to bubble for 1 minute, then keep hot.

Dip each pancake into the sauce on both sides, then fold in four and leave to one side of the pan or dish, to allow room to dip the others. When all the crêpes have been dipped and folded, and arranged in the pan, sprinkle with the caster sugar, heat the brandy, pour over and set alight, and bring the dish flaming to table.

Puréed Chestnuts

MONT BLANC

450g (1lb) chestnuts	60g (2oz) caster sugar
140ml ($\frac{1}{4}$ pint, $\frac{5}{8}$ cup US) milk	280ml ($\frac{1}{2}$ pint, 1$\frac{1}{4}$ cups US)
140ml ($\frac{1}{4}$ pint, $\frac{5}{8}$ cup US) water	double or whipping cream or
110g (4oz) granulated sugar	crème fraîche (see p. 16)
$\frac{1}{2}$ teaspoon vanilla essence, or	2 teaspoons icing sugar
vanilla pod	

Put the chestnuts in a large pan, cover with cold water, bring to the boil and boil for 10 minutes. Turn off the heat, take out the chestnuts a few at a time, and peel off the outer and inner skins.

Return chestnuts to a clean saucepan and add the milk and water. There should be just enough liquid to cover the chestnuts. Add the granulated sugar and the vanilla essence or pod and simmer very gently for 50–60 minutes, until all the liquid has evaporated and the chestnuts are quite tender.

Pass the chestnuts through a nylon sieve or the finest disk of a mouli or a mincer. Pile the fine strands of chestnut purée loosely into a mound on a serving dish, and sprinkle with the caster sugar.

Whip the cream lightly with the icing sugar. If you are using double cream or crème fraiche, add 2 tablespoons of cold water so that the cream remains very light. Smooth it gently over the pyramid of chestnuts with a palette knife, or pipe on, using a rosette nozzle.

Chocolate Mousse

MOUSSE AU CHOCOLAT

This should ideally be made the day before serving, and left to mature overnight.

200g (7oz) plain or bitter eating
chocolate
6 eggs

2 tablespoons brandy or Grand
Marnier or Orange Curaçao
(optional)

Break the chocolate into pieces and melt in a large basin over a pan of simmering water.

Remove from the heat and beat in the egg yolks one by one with a wooden spoon. Do not add the next yolk until the previous one has been thoroughly absorbed. The mixture will become stiff and dry at first, but persevere and it will gradually get smoother and softer.

Blend in the brandy or liqueur.

Beat the egg whites until they are stiff but not completely dry. Stir about $\frac{1}{3}$ of the egg whites into the chocolate mixture until they are completely blended in, then fold in the remaining egg whites lightly with a silver spoon or a spatula.

Pour into a glass or soufflé dish, and leave in the refrigerator or a cool place until ready to serve.

Foamy Liqueur Omelette

OMELETTE SOUFFLE GRAND MARNIER

This quantity is sufficient for a rich dessert for 2 people. It would be difficult for a cook-hostess to make more, as it must be eaten immediately.

3 medium or 2 large eggs　　　　*a walnut sized piece of butter*
30g (1oz) sugar　　　　　　　　*1 dessertspoon sifted icing sugar*
2 tablespoons Grand Marnier

Separate the eggs and beat the yolks with the sugar and one tablespoon of the Grand Marnier. Beat the whites till they stand in peaks, but are not quite dry. Fold into the yolks.

Heat a 25cm or 30cm (10in or 12in) omelette pan over a fairly high heat, take off the heat and put in the butter. Swirl round the pan, and as soon as it has melted but not changed colour, pour in the omelette mixture. Shake the pan a little, return to the heat and as the omelette begins to set, loosen the edge with a palette knife. When the bottom of the omelette seems cooked, but the centre is still very fluffy, slide half the omelette on to a heated plate, and fold over the other half. Sprinkle immediately with the icing sugar, pour over the second tablespoonful of Grand Marnier and set alight. Bring flaming to the table.

Individual Chocolate Creams

PETITS POTS DE CHOCOLAT

200g (7oz) plain or bitter eating　　*dash of salt*
　chocolate　　　　　　　　　　*3–4 drops vanilla essence* or
280ml (½ pint, 1¼ cups US)　　　　*1 teaspoon vanilla sugar*
　single cream　　　　　　　　　*1 egg*

Break up the chocolate into a small bowl. Scald the cream and pour it on to the chocolate. Stir with a wooden spoon till the chocolate has completely melted and the mixture is quite smooth. If necessary, set the bowl over a pan of simmering water and stir till smooth. Add the salt and vanilla, and lastly stir in the lightly beaten egg.

If you have an electric blender, break the chocolate into the blender jar, pour on the hot cream and blend till smooth. Blend in the remaining ingredients.

Pour into individual pots or ramekin dishes and chill for at least four hours before serving. The mixture will set to a smooth thick cream.

Serves 4 generously.

Profiteroles

For the puffs
280ml (½ pint, 1¼ cups US)
  water
100g (3½oz) butter
pinch of salt
1 teaspoon sugar
125g (4½oz) flour
4 eggs

For the filling
280ml (½ pint, 1¼ cups US)
  double or whipping cream
1 teaspoon icing sugar

For the sauce
140g (5oz) sugar
140ml (¼ pint, ⅝ cup US) water
1 tablespoon cocoa
60g (2oz) chocolate

Put the water with the butter, roughly cut into pieces, and the salt and sugar in a heavy saucepan and bring slowly to the boil. Stir until all the butter has melted. Sift the flour and pour it all into the pan. Lower the heat and beat with a wooden spoon for a minute or two, until the mixture forms a single thick, smooth mass and leaves the sides of the pan clean. Remove the pan from the heat and beat in the eggs, one by one, adding each one only when the previous one has been completely amalgamated. You should end up with a butter-yellow, smooth and glossy mixture, lukewarm and stiff enough to hold its shape.

Fill the mixture into a piping bag with a plain 1½cm (¾in) nozzle, and pipe small mounds on to buttered baking sheets, or drop small mounds of the mixture on to the baking sheets with a teaspoon. Leave plenty of space between each one to allow the puffs to rise.

Bake in the top of a hot oven (220C, 425F, Mark 7) for 20–25 minutes. They should be well risen and pale brown.

Remove from the oven and turn it off. Make an incision in the side of each puff with a sharp pointed knife and open them. Lay each on its side on the baking sheets and return to the oven to dry for 10 minutes, leaving the door open. Then leave to cool on a wire rack.

Whip the cream and icing sugar with a hand whisk until it is light but firm, and use a teaspoon to fill each puff generously with cream.

To make the sauce, bring the sugar, water and cocoa to the boil fiercely for 5 minutes. Remove from the heat, break in the chocolate and stir until the chocolate has melted and the sauce is quite smooth. Bring briefly to the boil again.

Pile the puffs into a dish, pour over the hot sauce and serve.

Variations

Croquembouches

Make cream puffs as for profiteroles above.

For the topping
155g (5½oz) sugar
2 tablespoons water
finely grated rind of ½ orange

For the filling
280ml (½ pint, 1¼ cups US)
double or whipping cream
1 teaspoon icing sugar
1 tablespoon Grand Marnier, or
Orange Curaçao
finely grated rind of 1 orange

Melt the sugar in a heavy saucepan with the water and the orange peel. When it turns a rich golden brown, remove from the heat and either dip each puff in the caramel, or pour a little of the caramel on to each puff. Leave to dry and harden.

Whip the cream with the icing sugar, using a hand whisk, until it begins to become bulky. Slowly whip in the Grand Marnier or Orange Curaçao and the orange rind, and whip

until light but firm. Fill each puff with this mixture. Pile into
a dish and serve.

Gâteau Saint-Honore

To make a simple version of this traditional French birthday
cake, pipe the choux pastry in a circle, about 2½cm (1in)
thick, on to a buttered baking sheet and make puffs with the
remaining pastry on to a separate, buttered baking sheet.
(There should be at least one puff for each year of the birthday, so double the quantities if necessary.) Cook as above,
allowing an extra 5–10 minutes baking time for the ring.

When the puffs have been dipped in the syrup and allowed
to dry, arrange them in a circle on the top of the ring, using a
little more syrup to attach them. Fill the centre of the ring
with whipped cream, decorate, if you like, with candied
fruits, and place a cake candle in the centre of each puff.

Hot Chocolate Soufflé

SOUFFLE AU CHOCOLAT

100g (3½oz) plain or bitter chocolate	30g (1oz) cornflour
	60g (2oz) sugar
2 tablespoons water	3 egg yolks
2 teaspoons instant coffee (optional)	5 egg whites
	pinch of salt
250ml (scant ½ pint, 1¼ cups US) milk	1 tablespoon caster sugar
	1 tablespoon icing sugar

Butter a 1 litre (2 pint) soufflé dish generously, and sprinkle
bottom and sides with a little of the sugar.

Melt the chocolate over gentle heat together with the
water, adding the instant coffee if you like. Stir well and cook
a little to allow the chocolate to thicken.

Mix the cornflour to a smooth thin paste with a little of the
milk.

Add remaining milk gradually to the chocolate, stirring till it dissolves, add the sugar, pour in the cornflour paste, stir well, bring to the boil and boil for one minute.

Remove from the heat and beat in the egg yolks one by one.

Whip the whites together with the pinch of salt, and when they begin to become grainy, add the caster sugar and whip again until they stand in peaks.

Stir about one-third of the egg whites into the chocolate sauce and blend until smooth. Gently fold in the remaining egg whites.

Pour into the prepared soufflé dish, and place immediately into a preheated moderately hot oven (190C, 375F, Mark 5) and cook for 40 minutes.

Sprinkle the soufflé, which should by now have risen and started to form a pale gold crust, with a little of the sifted icing sugar. Return to the oven, and repeat three or four times in the next 5 minutes, as soon as the icing sugar has melted. This must be done very quickly, and will give the soufflé a transparent glaze.

Bring the soufflé to table immediately.

Hot Orange Liqueur Soufflé

SOUFFLE AU GRAND MARNIER

60g (2oz) cornflour	45g (1½oz) butter
250ml (scant ½ pint, 1¼ cups US) milk	2 tablespoons Grand Marnier
110g (4oz) sugar	4 egg yolks
1 teaspoon vanilla sugar or 6 drops vanilla essence	6 egg whites
3 sugar lumps	pinch of salt
1 orange	1 tablespoon caster sugar
	1 tablespoon icing sugar

Butter 1 litre (2 pint) soufflé dish generously and sprinkle the bottom and sides with a little of the sugar.

Mix the cornflour to a smooth thin paste with a little of the milk.

Bring the remaining milk, together with the rest of the sugar and the vanilla sugar or essence gently to just below boiling point. Rub the sugar lumps well over the orange until they become impregnated with the oil from the orange skin and add these to the milk. Stir until dissolved. Pour in the cornflour paste, stir well and bring gently to the boil. Boil for one minute, stirring constantly, until a thick smooth sauce has been obtained. Remove from the heat, cut the butter into small pieces and blend in, piece by piece, until the butter is melted and the sauce becomes glossy. Add the Grand Marnier.

Separate the eggs and beat the yolks one by one into the sauce.

Whip the whites with the pinch of salt until they are stiff. When they begin to become grainy, add the caster sugar and whip again.

Stir about one-third of the egg whites into the sauce, and then gently fold in the remainder.

Pour into the prepared soufflé dish, and place immediately into a moderately hot preheated oven (180C, 350F, Mark 4) and cook for 35 minutes.

Sprinkle the soufflé, which should by now have risen and started to form a pale gold crust, with a little of the sifted icing sugar. Return to the oven, and repeat three or four times in the next 5 minutes, as soon as the icing sugar has melted. This must be done very quickly, and will give the soufflé a transparent glaze.

Bring the soufflé to table immediately.

Apple Sorbet with Apple Brandy

SORBET DE POMMES AU CALVADOS

In very grand restaurants in Normandy, this is sometimes served between the fish and the meat course, to revive the jaded appetite. However it makes a quite delicious enough dessert for the end of a rich meal, with or without the apple brandy. As the apples do not need to be peeled, it is an ideal use for windfalls.

700g (1½lb) apples, cooking or
  eating
140ml (¼ pint, ⅝ cup US) water
170g (6oz) sugar

2 egg whites
2–4 tablespoons calvados (apple
  brandy)

Quarter the apples and remove the stalks and any damaged parts, but do not bother to peel or core. Put in a heavy saucepan with a few tablespoons of water and cook over a moderate heat until soft. Stir from time to time and if necessary add a little more water to stop the apples catching. When the apples are quite soft, pass through a food mouli or a nylon sieve. You should have about 420ml (¾ pint, 1⅞ cups US) of purée.

Boil the water with the sugar for 5 minutes. Stir this syrup into the apple purée, pour into metal freezing trays and freeze, either in the ice-making compartment of the refrigerator, set to its coldest setting, or in the freezer. When the mixture is almost set, beat it with a rotary or electric beater. Whip the egg whites until they are stiff and fold into the mixture. Return to the refrigerator or freezer.

Before the meal, chill a wine glass or an individual glass dessert bowl for each person, and spoon in the sorbet. Return to the refrigerator or freezer until ready to serve.

Pour a little calvados into each glass at the table.

French Apple Tart

TARTE NORMANDE

225g (8oz) pâte brisée sucrée (approx. ½ quantity given on p. 19)
140ml (¼ pint, ⅝ cup US) water (approx.)

1kg (2lb) cooking apples
30g (1oz) butter
60g (2oz) sugar (approx.)
2 tablespoons marmalade, apricot jam or apple jelly

Line a 30cm (12in) loose-bottomed flan tin with the pastry and bake blind for 10 minutes in a hot oven (220C, 425F, Mark 7).

Set aside 2 or 3 large apples (approximately 500g, 1lb). Peel, core and chop the remaining apples and cook until soft in just enough water to stop them catching. When they are cooked to a purée, beat in the butter and sugar to taste (approximately 30g, 1oz). Spread this purée evenly into the pastry case.

Peel, quarter and core the remaining apples and cut into transparently thin half-moon slices. Lay these, overlapping, in concentric circles over the top of the apple purée, so that the whole tart is covered with the apple slices. Sprinkle on the remaining sugar and return to the oven for a further 20–25 minutes. When cooked, the edges of the apple slices should be just darkened.

When the tart has cooled, melt the marmalade, jam or jelly in a small saucepan, adding a little water to marmalade or jam, strain and glaze the tart. Leave to set before serving with whipped cream or crème chantilly (see p. 17).

Hot Apple Tarts

TARTES A POMMES CHAUDES

250g (8oz) puff pastry　　　　　　*30g (1oz) butter*
4 well flavoured eating apples　　　*60g (2oz) caster sugar*
*　(Cox Orange Pippins are*　　　　*140ml (¼ pint, ⅝ cup US)*
*　especially good)*　　　　　　　　*　calvados*

Roll out the pastry about ¼cm (⅛in) thick, and cut out into four circles. With the sharp point of a kitchen knife mark a circle 1cm (½in) in from the edge.

Peel and core the apples, and cut each one into eighths.

Brush the pastry circles with half the butter, arrange eight apple slices on each in a flower-like shape, keeping inside the marked line. Brush with the remaining butter and sprinkle with half the sugar.

Cook in a hot oven (230C, 450F, Mark 8) for 20–25 minutes. The edges of the apples should just begin to turn dark brown, the pastry should have formed a kind of nest round the apples.

Heat the calvados in a small saucepan. Put the apple tarts on a heated dish, sprinkle with the remaining sugar, pour a little of the heated calvados over each tart and set alight immediately. Bring flaming to the table. Serve with some thick cream or crème chantilly. (See p. 17.)

Plum Tart

TARTE A PRUNES

This should be made with the yellow-fleshed, bloom-covered, purple-skinned plums known in this country as sviters or by their German name, Zwetschgen.

200g (7oz) pâte brisée sucrée　　*450g (1lb) plums*
*　(half the quantity given on p.*　　*60g (2oz) sugar*
*　19)*

Line a 23cm or 25cm (9in or 10in) flan tin with the pastry,

prick well and bake blind in a moderately hot oven (170C, 375F, Mark 5) for 10 minutes, until it is pale brown.

Wash, halve and stone the plums, then lay them, cut side down, in circles on the pastry. Sprinkle with the sugar and return to the oven for 20–30 minutes, until the plums look soft and very juicy.

Serve hot or cold, but very fresh, with crème chantilly (see p. 17) if you like.

Upside Down Apple Tart

TARTE TATIN

200g (7oz) pâte brisée sucrée (half the quantity given on p. 19)	60g (2oz) butter 110g (4oz) sugar 750g (1½lb) tart cooking apples

Butter a 22cm (9in) flan tin thickly with half the butter, and sprinkle with half the sugar. Peel and core the apples, cut into very thick slices (8–12 slices per apple) and arrange these closely together in concentric circles in the flan case. Place the case over a high but even heat for 5 minutes, to melt and caramelise the butter and sugar. Remove from the heat, dot with the remaining butter and sprinkle with the remaining sugar.

Roll the pastry into a circle the size of the flan tin and place over the apples, allowing the edges to fall just inside the tin. Make several incisions into the pastry with a sharp knife to allow steam to escape.

Bake in a moderately hot oven (200C, 400F, Mark 6) for 35–40 minutes, until the top is golden brown.

Allow to cool a little before carefully inverting on to a large dish. Serve warm or cold.

Cakes and Pastries
•
Les Gâteaux et Patisseries

The mouthwatering array of beautifully decorated cakes, small and large, which are to be found in French patisserie shops, must be a considerable discouragement to homebaking, and the more elaborate concoctions are probably best left to the patissier. However, there are many simple cakes and pastries, some of them regional, which can very well be made at home.

I have included recipes for brioche and croissants, which it is unlikely that a French housewife would attempt to make herself. Although these can also be bought in this country, they tend to be very expensive, and it is well worth making them occasionally for a Sunday morning breakfast treat.

Finally, there are recipes for a couple of bonnes bouches, simply because I could not bear to leave them out.

Brioche

This is not difficult to make, but takes time and cannot be hurried.

15g ($\frac{1}{2}$oz) yeast
70ml ($\frac{1}{8}$ pint, $\frac{1}{4}$ cup US) water
pinch of sugar
225g (8oz) plain strong white
  flour
pinch of salt
100g (3$\frac{1}{2}$oz) unsalted butter

2 eggs
1 tablespoon caster sugar

For the glaze
1 tablespoon milk
1 tablespoon sugar

Blend the water and sugar into the yeast, cover and leave in a warm place until frothy.

Sift the flour and salt into a large bowl and rub in the softened butter until the mixture resembles fine breadcrumbs.

Beat the eggs together lightly with the sugar.

Make a well in the centre of the flour and pour in the yeast and the eggs and work into the flour, first with a wooden spoon, then using your hands.

You should have a light springy dough, but still quite soft and sticky. Cover and leave to rise in a warm place for 3–4 hours, until the dough has doubled in bulk.

Knead the dough down again, and put in a clean bowl, covered, or in a polythene bag, loosely tied. Leave overnight in the bottom part of the refrigerator, or in a cool place.

In the morning, knead down again and prepare for baking.

Use one large well-buttered, fluted brioche tin, or 10–12 individual ones. If you do not have a brioche tin, use a ring mould or castle pudding tins. Fill the mould $\frac{2}{3}$ of the way up, then make a deep circular cut in the top. This will allow the dough to rise to the traditional top knot. Or roll $\frac{3}{4}$ of the dough into 10–12 round balls, and place them on a buttered baking sheet. Slightly flatten the tops. Roll the remaining dough into an equal number of smaller balls, pinch them to a point at one end. With your thumb, make a deep indentation in the centre of each of the larger balls, and fit in the stalks of the little ones.

Leave to rise again in a warm place for half an hour.

Bake in a hot oven (230C, 450F, Mark 8) for 20–25 minutes, until they are risen and very faintly browned on top.

Meanwhile boil the milk and sugar together until the mixture thickens. Paint the tops of the brioches liberally with this glaze and return to the oven for 2–3 minutes, for the glaze to set. Serve very fresh.

Variation

Brioches can also be served with savouries. For this the caster sugar should be omitted from the ingredients, and a milk and egg glaze should be used instead of the sweet one given above.

Individual brioches, served hot, with the centre hollowed out and filled with a smooth pâté, such as the pâté de foie de volaille given on p. 32 and the top replaced, make a wonderful first course.

Croissants

35g (good 1oz) yeast	*200g (7oz) butter*
4 tablespoons warm water	*500g (good 1lb) flour*
25g (1oz) sugar	*2 teaspoons salt*
280ml ($\frac{1}{2}$ pint, $1\frac{1}{4}$ cups US)	*1 egg yolk*
* milk*	*2 tablespoons milk*

Dissolve the yeast in the warm water, and add 1 teaspoon of the sugar. Leave in a warm place till frothy (10–15 minutes). Scald the milk, remove from the heat and add 30g (1oz) of the butter and the rest of the sugar. Stir till dissolved, and leave till lukewarm. Sift the flour and salt into a basin, make a well in the centre and when it is ready pour in the yeast mixture and then the milk and butter mixture, and work into the flour with a wooden spoon. Knead the mixture until it is smooth and springy, and leaves the sides of the bowl clean. Cover with a clean cloth and leave in a warm place to rise, until the dough has at least doubled its bulk.

Soften the remaining butter on a plate until it is quite soft and smooth, but do not allow it to become runny.

When the dough is ready, knock down and knead on a floured surface, then roll out into a rectangle three times as long as it is wide. Spread one-third of the softened butter on two-thirds of the rectangle, fold over the unbuttered third and then fold over the top. Seal the edges, give the pastry a half turn and roll out again into a rectangle. Fold over three times as before, and leave in the refrigerator for $\frac{1}{2}$ hour to rest. Repeat this operation twice more until all the butter has been used. Leave the dough to rest in the refrigerator for 1 hour.

Roll out the dough on a floured surface into a large rectangle, rather less than $\frac{1}{2}$cm ($\frac{1}{4}$in) thick. Cut into squares 10–15cm (4–6in) wide, depending on how large you want your croissants. Cut each square into two triangles. Roll each triangle from the wide edge to the point, place on an unbuttered baking tray, with the point underneath, and form into crescent shape. Brush with the egg yolk beaten in the 2 tablespoons of milk.

Bake for 15–20 minutes at 190C (375F, Mark 5).

Once shaped, the crescents can be kept in the refrigerator overnight, for baking fresh for breakfast, but they must be left out at room temperature for at least $\frac{1}{2}$ hour before baking.

They can also be stored unbaked in the freezer, but should be left for at least 1 hour at room temperature before baking.

Eclairs

For the éclairs
280ml (½ pint, 1¼ cups US)
  water
100g (3½oz) butter
pinch of salt
1 teaspoon sugar
125g (4½oz) flour
4 eggs

For the filling
140ml (¼ pint, ⅝ cup US) double
  or whipping cream
1 teaspoon icing sugar

For the icing
4 tablespoons water
1 tablespoon sugar
60g (2oz) plain or bitter eating
  chocolate
1 teaspoon powdered coffee
100g (3½oz) icing sugar
½ teaspoon corn or salad oil

Put the water with the butter, roughly cut into pieces, and the salt and sugar in a heavy saucepan and bring slowly to the boil. Stir until all the butter has melted. Sift the flour and pour it all into the pan. Lower the heat and beat with a wooden spoon for a minute or two, until the mixture forms a single thick, smooth mass and leaves the sides of the pan clean. Remove the pan from the heat and beat in the eggs, one by one, adding each one only when the previous one has been completely amalgamated. You should end up with a butter-yellow, smooth and glossy mixture, lukewarm and stiff enough to hold its shape.

Fill the mixture into a piping bag with a plain 1cm (½in) nozzle, and pipe finger-sized éclairs on to buttered baking sheets, leaving plenty of space between each one. The éclairs should be slightly stumpy at each end.

Bake in the top of a hot oven (220C, 425F, Mark 7) for 20–25 minutes. They should be well risen and pale brown.

Remove from the oven and turn it off. Make an incision down the side of each éclair with a sharp, pointed knife to allow the air to escape, lay them on their sides on the baking sheets and return to the oven to dry for 10 minutes, leaving the oven door open. Then leave to cool on a wire rack.

Whip the cream and icing sugar with a hand whisk until it

is light but firm, and fill the éclairs, using a knife, teaspoon or the piping bag.

To make the icing put the water and sugar in a small saucepan and bring slowly to the boil, stirring until the sugar has dissolved. Boil quite briskly for 1 minute. Remove from the heat and break in the chocolate. Stir until dissolved. Add the coffee and slowly beat in the icing sugar, keeping the mixture gently warm. Stir in the oil.

Using a knife, coat the top of each éclair thickly with the chocolate icing and leave to dry before serving.

Breton Cake

GATEAU BRETON

Slices of this cake can be bought from market or street stalls in Brittany. It is both rich and dry, excellent eaten with tea or coffee, or, as in Brittany, with a glass of cider.

340g (12oz) flour	*6 egg yolks*
170g (6oz) sugar	*200g (7oz) butter*

Sift the flour and sugar together into a bowl and make a well in the centre. Whisk 5 egg yolks together with a fork, pour into the centre of the bowl and slowly work in the flour with a wooden spoon to start with, then crumble together with the finger tips till the mixture resembles fine breadcrumbs. Cut the butter, which should be fairly soft, into small pieces, and, using a palette knife at first, then finger tips, work into the flour until the mixture resembles a rich, crumbly pastry.

Press into a well-buttered 22cm (9in) flan tin, paint the remaining egg yolk over the top and cook in a moderately hot oven (190C, 375F, Mark 5) for 1 hour.

Puff Pastry and Almond Cake

GATEAU DE PITHIVIERS

2 eggs
140g (5oz) sugar
100g (3½oz) ground almonds
100g (3½oz) butter

1 tablespoon brandy or Kirsch
368g (13oz) puff pastry
1 tablespoon icing sugar

Beat the eggs together, then slowly beat in the sugar and almonds. Add the softened butter, a little at a time, and continue to beat the mixture until it is light and fluffy. Beat in the brandy or Kirsch.

Cut the pastry into two unequal halves. Roll out the larger to 1cm (approximately ⅜in) thick, and, using a plate or flan tin, cut a circle 22cm (9in) diameter. Add the trimmings to the remaining pastry.

Place the circle on a dampened baking sheet, and prick well with a fork. Spread the almond mixture on this, leaving a 2cm (1in) margin all round.

Roll out the second piece of pastry to make a bigger circle (approximately 25cm (10in) diameter).

Moisten the edges of both circles and place the second one, moistened side down, on top of the first.

Press down the edges firmly and crimp to seal. Make a number of incisions in a decorative pattern in the top to allow the steam to escape.

Place in a moderately hot oven (190C, 375F, Mark 5) and bake for 35–40 minutes, until the top begins to colour. Then raise the heat to (260C, 500F, Mark 9) and sprinkle on a little of the sifted icing sugar. As soon as this begins to melt, sprinkle on a little more and continue until all the icing sugar has been used. This will give a fine glaze to the top of the cake.

Serve very fresh.

Madeleines

Traditionally these little cakes, immortalised by Proust, should be baked in fluted shell-shaped tins, but if these are not available small bun or patty tins will also do.

2 large eggs, or 3 smaller
170g (6oz) sugar
170g (6oz) butter, preferably
   unsalted

1 tablespoon lemon juice
170g (6oz) flour

Separate the eggs and whisk the yolks with the sugar until they are pale and fluffy. Beat in the softened butter and the lemon juice. When the mixture is light and smooth, gradually blend in the sifted flour. Break up the egg whites lightly with a fork and beat these into the mixture.

Drop large teaspoonfuls into buttered madeleine or patty tins and bake in a moderate oven (160C, 325F, Mark 3) for 20–25 minutes, until they just begin to brown round the edges.

These cakes should be eaten very fresh when they are crisp and quite dry, and are delicious dunked in tea. They can also be frozen and eaten within ½ hour of emerging from the freezer.

Variation

Four Part Cake

GATEAU QUATRE QUARTS

To make this delicately light, plain cake use the ingredients and follow instructions as for Madeleines, but whisk the egg whites till they stand in soft peaks before folding into the mixture. Pour into a buttered 20cm (8in) cake tin and cook in a moderately hot oven (190C, 375F, Mark 5) for 1 hour.

Almond Biscuits

TUILES

These crisp little biscuits are lightly curved to resemble the
Provençal roof tiles from which they take their name. They
can be made plain or with almonds (in which case they become
tuiles d'amandes) and may be eaten alone with a cup of tea
or coffee, or served instead of wafers with ice-cream, or with
a compote of fruit.

30g (1oz) butter
100g (3½oz) plain flour
pinch of salt
140g (5oz) caster sugar

225g (8oz) flaked almonds
(optional)
5 eggs

Melt the butter and leave to cool.

Sift the flour, salt and sugar into a basin. If you are using
the flaked almonds, roast them lightly first in a moderate oven,
or under the grill, then add to the flour and sugar in the basin.

Beat the eggs together lightly with a fork, then blend slowly
into the flour mixture. Finally add the melted butter.

Drop small teaspoonfuls of the mixture on to buttered
baking sheets, leaving plenty of space between, as the biscuits
spread. Cook in a hot oven (220C, 425F, Mark 7) for 10
minutes, by which time they should be thin and flat and golden
in the centre, brown at the edges.

Remove from the oven, and immediately take each tuile off
the baking sheet with a palette knife and drape it over a
rolling pin, pressing down gently so that they take the lightly
rounded shape. Leave on a rack to finish cooling; they will
become quite crisp as they cool.

Sugared Chestnuts

MARRONS GLACES

1kg (2lb) chestnuts	*1¼ litres (2½ pints, 6¼ cups US)*
1 tablespoon lemon juice	*water*
500g (1lb) sugar	

Put the chestnuts in a large pan, cover with cold water, bring to the boil and boil for 2 minutes. Turn off the heat, take out the chestnuts a few at a time, and peel off outer and inner skin. Drop peeled chestnuts into a bowl of cold water to which you have added the lemon juice. If the chestnuts become difficult to peel, bring briefly to the boil again.

Melt the sugar in the 1¼ litres (2½ pints, 6¼ cups US) fresh water, and boil for 20 minutes. Drain the chestnuts and drop them gently into the syrup. Bring back to just below boiling point and simmer for 10 minutes. Pour into a bowl and leave to stand overnight.

The following day drain off the syrup and boil for 10 minutes. Slide the chestnuts carefully into the syrup, bring back to boiling point and take off the heat. Allow to stand again overnight.

Repeat this operation once more.

Take the chestnuts out of the syrup after they have soaked in it overnight for the last time, drain well and place them on foil-lined baking sheets. Dry in a very low oven or overnight in an airing cupboard.

Bring the remaining syrup to the boil and boil until very thick, but do not allow to brown. Pour very slowly over each chestnut until it has all been used up. Leave to dry and harden.

Store the marrons glacés in airtight jars, in the refrigerator or freezer. Serve as confectionery, or use to decorate ices, gâteaux and other desserts. Broken fragments may be folded into brandy flavoured whipped cream or ice cream to make a simple but rich dessert.

Chocolate Truffles

TRUFFLES NAPOLEON

280ml (½ pint, 1¼ cups US)
  double cream
340g (12oz) plain or bitter
  chocolate

1 teaspoon coffee powder
100g (3½oz) unsalted butter
1 tablespoon brandy
30g (1oz) cocoa

Bring the cream to the boil and simmer for 5 minutes.

Meanwhile melt the chocolate in the top of a double boiler, or in a basin set over a pan of simmering water. Add the coffee and stir well till smooth.

Add the chocolate to the cream and stir over a low heat until the mixture is absolutely smooth and begins to thicken. Leave to set in the refrigerator overnight.

The next day melt the chocolate cream gently in the top of the double boiler, or in a basin set over a pan of simmering water. Add the butter, bit by bit, and stir each time so that the butter is absorbed. Do not heat the mixture more than is necessary to allow the butter to just melt and be amalgamated.

Leave to cool. Add the brandy and when the mixture begins to set, whisk with a rotary whisk or electric beater for at least 10 minutes till it becomes light and fluffy.

Chill for 3–4 hours to firm, then form into ball or sausage shapes and roll in the cocoa. Refrigerate overnight before eating. Keep refrigerated.

Index

By the same author

THE PENGUIN FREEZER COOKBOOK
(*with Sheila Bush*)
also published in hardback as
A FREEZER FOR ALL SEASONS

ICES GALORE (*with Sheila Bush*)